# Cambridge Latin Course

# Book IV

## Teacher's Guide

## FOURTH EDITION

**UNIVERSITY OF CAMBRIDGE**
**SCHOOL CLASSICS PROJECT**

PUBLISHED BY THE UNIVERSITY OF CAMBRIDGE SCHOOL CLASSICS PROJECT,
3 Bene't Place, Cambridge CB2 1EL, United Kingdom.

http://www.cambridgescp.com

This book, an outcome of work jointly commissioned by the Schools Council before its closure and the Cambridge School Classics Project, is published under the aegis of Qualifications and Curriculum Authority Enterprises Limited, 29 Bolton Stgreet, London W1Y 7PD.

First published 1973
Second edition 1985
This edition 2003

Printed in the United Kingdom by Larman Printers, Cambridge

ISBN 0-9542794-3-3

Illustration by Simon Armour

# ACKNOWLEDGEMENTS

For help in preparing Book IV of the *Cambridge Latin Course* and this Teacher's Guide we should like to express our thanks to the following: Jill Dalladay for her extensive revision of the Guide; members of the Project's Working Party: Eileen Emmett, Jean Hubbard and Pam Perkins; Robin Griffin, revision editor of the 2nd edition, for his expert advice and many stimulating suggestions for teaching method; Maire Collins for typing and formatting the text; and for assistance of various kinds: Patricia Acres, Simon Armour, Roger Davies, Lynda Goss, William Horbury, Debbie James, John Patterson, Tony Smith and Meg Thorpe.

Bob Lister, Director

Pat Story, Revision Editor

Roger Dalladay, Picture Editor

# CONTENTS

# Cambridge Latin Course Book IV

| Stage | Name | Cultural background | Main language features |
|---|---|---|---|
| 29 | **Rōma** | The Forum Romanum, heart of Rome and the empire. The dedication of the arch of Titus commemorating the conquest of Judaea. | Present and imperfect passive (3rd person singular and plural). Purpose clauses introduced by **quī** and **ubi**. |
| 30 | **Haterius** | Roman building techniques. | Perfect passive. Pluperfect passive. |
| 31 | **in urbe** | The city of Rome, its splendour and squalor. Patronage: duties of patrons and clients; the **salūtātiō**. | Ablative absolute. **nē** in indirect commands and purpose clauses. |
| 32 | **Euphrosynē** | The structure of Roman society. Some Roman popular beliefs: astrology, Stoicism and Mithraism. | Deponent verbs. Gerundives of obligation. Future participles. |
| 33 | **pantomīmus** | Christianity. Entertainment: theatre, chariot-racing, gladiatorial fights, private entertainment. | Future active. Future perfect active. |
| 34 | **lībertus** | Freedmen. | Present passive infinitive. Future passive (3rd person singular and plural). |

# INTRODUCTION

This book provides guidelines for teaching Stages 29-34 and information about the text and illustrations in the student's book.

Book IV is set in Rome. It describes the physical appearance of the city and examines various aspects of Roman life including the class system, patronage, religious and philosophical beliefs and popular entertainments. The story line takes as its starting-point the dedication of the arch of Titus commemorating the conquest of the Jews and then follows two of the main characters, Salvius and the contractor Haterius, through episodes ranging from a bizarre birthday party to the violent end of the empress' favourite.

The events of Stages 29 and 30 are set in AD 81, Stages 31 and 32 take place in AD 82, and Stages 33 and 34 in AD 83. (Book II was set in AD 82 and Book III in AD 83.)

The aims and principles of the *Cambridge Latin Course* are explained in the Book I Teacher's Guide. This introduction attempts to reflect on some of the questions which arise for many teachers in the later Stages of the Course: What are the implications of a reading course at this level? How can the Course be used as preparation for GSCE? What are the needs of the minority of students going on to AS and A2 and how can they be catered for effectively in the context of a varied group? How can the final parts of the Course be managed in the time available?

The suggestions made in this Introduction and the Stage commentaries should be regarded as a bank of ideas from which teachers should select only what is relevant and possible in their particular circumstances. We know that many are subject to severe constraints of time.

## 1 Reading

The aim of the *Cambridge Latin Course* is to develop fluency and appreciation in reading Latin in the original. It is therefore important to:

> ensure that every lesson contains some reading of Latin;
> use the Latin text as the starting-point for all work on language, both the introduction of new points and the consolidation of old features;
> continue to use reading aloud and comprehension questions as the main tools for approaching a story and unravelling complex sentences;
> apply the techniques of literary criticism, giving due regard to the sound of the Latin; the writer's effectiveness and his use of stylistic features to develop plot, character and atmosphere;
> relate the reading material to students' own interests and to other subjects in the curriculum.

*Variety* in the range of reading material and the approaches used is important, e.g.:

a   Re-use of earlier material promotes fluency. In relation to a recurring theme (e.g. Salvius' attitude to different people and situations) re-read (or recall) an earlier incident, in connection with a new story; or ask students to find in a previous story examples of a language feature about to be developed further, or vocabulary that will recur in the new passage. Returning to an earlier story which students can easily manage is also morale-boosting if they have hit a hard patch; it is an effective way of demonstrating to them that they actually have made progress.

b   Use easy or less important new material to build student confidence. Let students read it on their own and provide a bank of written or taped translations so that they have a means of checking.

c   Encourage a range of responses to a passage to stimulate imagination and versatility, e.g.: sketch, enact, summarise, read in Latin with appropriate expression, translate orally in groups or individually, prepare or translate a passage not seen before; answer comprehension questions; pick out and analyse words which describe character, or action, or atmosphere.

d   Select significant passages for study in depth to develop literary appreciation. Discuss content and style, examining the language and imagery used, eliciting a range of acceptable translations and discussing the effect of differences in the style of translation.

*Discussion* is a natural response to any reading material. Even when time is short it should be used to increase the involvement and appreciation of students. When you are drawing attention to particular points of language or cultural background, you will be seeking correct answers or acceptable possibilities. Discussing a range of translations is more open-ended, and helps students to become sensitive to nuances in both languages. Topics such as religion, marriage, the use and abuse of power, the place of women - or slaves, or writers - in society, can strongly engage students and enable their Latin to make a contribution to their work in citizenship, or religious and moral education. Sometimes spontaneous discussion of last night's TV news or current films can illuminate Roman background and literature and reveal insights; at other times it is sufficient to highlight the issues raised in the passage just before the end of the lesson and leave students to discuss them on their own.

*Outside the classroom.* Encourage students to read around the subject, as reading in English extends their vocabulary, their general fluency and their linguistic sensitivity. Give them a reading list and ensure that the school library has a good stock of historical novels, attractive books about the themes covered in the course, good translations (especially of Ovid, Virgil, Catullus, Pliny and Tacitus), and audio-visual and computer materials. Consult the Cambridge School Classics Project website: www.cambridgescp.com, which lists resources.

## 2 Consolidation

Reading that is both accurate and fluent can be achieved only by systematic and regular consolidation of language features and vocabulary. This is much more effective than the occasional cramming of the contents of the 'Language information' section or the complete checklist vocabulary, which in the later books of the Course are likely to overwhelm and demoralise students by their sheer bulk.

By this stage in the Course you and your students will probably have favourite Latin phrases to trigger memory of particular words and language features. It is still worthwhile to continue adding phrases to the collection and to learn them by heart.

*Language features*

Consolidation should usually be undertaken in connection with the stories and detailed suggestions are made in the Stage commentaries. The following conspectus of these suggestions could form the basis of a general revision programme.

Note that some stories provide scope for the revision of several language points and that some of these occur more than once. Again, feel free to select only those suggestions that meet the needs and circumstances of your students. The same applies to the exercises in the Stages and those in the Language information. However, there may be occasions when you will need to provide examples to revise points not covered in the conspectus nor in the exercises in the text book; again, these are best based on the material in the stories.

It is important to maintain the pace and flow of a story and thus keep up the student's interest. Allocate a special time for consolidation and vary the ways in which it is done. Some points may require only a few minutes of oral work; others may involve a written exercise or a formal test.

*Suggestions for consolidation based on stories*

| Stage | Language feature | Story | Practising the language | Language information |
|---|---|---|---|---|
| 29 | 4th declension (also Stage 32) | nox I Masada I arcus Titī I | | p. 114, para. 1 |
| | Ablative (also Stages 30, 31, 33) | Masada I | | pp. 114-15, 135, para. 6 |
| | Personal and reflexive pronouns (also Stage 34) | Masada I and II | | p. 120 |
| | 5th declension (also Stage 32) | arcus Titī I | | p. 114, para. 1 |
| | Participles (also Stages 33, 34) | arcus Titī II | Ex. 2, p. 14 (present participles) | pp. 129, 130, 136, paras 1-3 |
| 30 | Irregular verbs | dignitās | | pp. 132-3 |
| | Comparatives and superlatives | dignitās | | pp. 118-19 |
| | Perfect and pluperfect active | dignitās | | p. 125 |
| | Cases of the noun, especially the ablative | polyspaston I | | pp. 114-15, 135 |

| Stage | Language feature | Story | Practising the language | Language information |
|---|---|---|---|---|
| 31 | Passive verbs (also Stages 33, 34) | **adventus** **salūtātiō II** | Ex. 1, p. 49 | pp. 126-7 |
| | Ablative of time | **salūtātiō I** | | p. 135, para. 6 |
| | Dative | **salūtātiō II** | | pp. 114-15, 135, para 5, 136-7, para. 5 |
| | Imperatives (also Stage 34) | **salūtātiō II** | | p. 128, para. 3 |
| | Gerundives (impersonal) | **salūtātiō II** | | |
| 32 | **is, īdem** | **Euphrosynē revocāta II** | | p. 122 |
| | Subjunctives and their uses (also Stage 33) | **cēna Hateriī** | Ex. 2, p. 69 (indirect commands) | p. 128, para. 1 pp. 138-9, paras 1-6 |
| | Ablative absolute (also Stage 33) | **cēna Hateriī** | | p. 136, para. 4 |
| | Genitive | **cēna Hateriī** | | pp. 114-15, 135, para. 4 |
| | **ferō** and compounds | **cēna Hateriī** | | pp. 132-4, 48 'Word patterns' |
| | 4th and 5th declension nouns | **philosophia** | | pp. 114-15 |
| | Selected pronouns | **philosophia** | | pp. 120-2 |
| 33 | Subjunctives and their uses | **Tychicus** | | pp. 138-9, paras 1-6 |
| | Perfect passive (and deponent) | **Tychicus** | | pp. 127, 130 |
| | Ablative, including ablative absolute | **Tychicus** | Ex. 1, p. 87 | pp. 114-15, 136, para. 4 |
| | Participial phrases | **Tychicus** | | pp. 136-7 |
| | Passive verbs | **in aulā Domitiānī I** | Ex. 2 p. 87 | pp. 126-7 |
| | Relative clauses | **in aulā Domitiānī II** | | p. 123 |

| Stage | Language feature | Story | Practising the language | Language information |
|---|---|---|---|---|
| 34 | Personal pronouns | **ultiō Epaphrodītī** | | p. 120 |
| | Present active infinitives | **ultiō Epaphrodītī** | | p. 128 |
| | Participles, including deponent | **īnsidiae I, exitium I** | | pp. 129, 130, 136-7 |
| | Imperatives and prohibitions | **exitium I** | | p. 128 |
| | Longer sentences | **exitium II** | | p. 140 |

*Vocabulary*
New words are, like linguistic points, best discussed in the context of a story; consolidation of 'old' vocabulary may conveniently take place before or after reading a passage, e.g. students are required to provide the translation of one word, the rest of the sentence being recalled by the teacher: **Titum vīvum ōderat**: *He hated Titus* **vīvum**. If the teacher notes down during the course of a lesson the words students have forgotten, this list could be used as a quick test. Students enjoy producing their own vocabulary quizzes, often subjecting the opposing team to more difficult words than their teacher would have selected.

The checklist vocabularies at the end of the Stages lend themselves to the following activities (examples are taken from the Stage 29 checklist):

* discussion of derivatives
* practice with cognates, especially those that have appeared or will appear in other checklist vocabularies, e.g. **audācia**: 'What is the meaning of **audāx**? **audēre**?
* using key parts of nouns and verbs, e.g. **captīvus**: 'What case is **captīvum**? **captīvōs**? What does this sentence mean: **vīta captīvōrum miserrima erat**? What case is **captīvōrum**?
* practice with compounds, e.g. 'If **circumveniō** means *I come around, I surround*, what do the following mean: **ēveniō, reveniō**?'
* sorting pairs of words of similar or opposite meanings, one of the pair to be in a particular checklist vocabulary, e.g. 'Find the pairs of opposites in the following list and give their meanings: **ascendō, mortuus, ōdī, salūs, dēscendō, perīculum, noster, vīvus, amō, vester**.'

## 4 Omitted material

The amount of reading material outstrips the time available for many groups. Decisions about what to omit should take into account not only linguistic features but also content and literary value, to ensure that reading remains enjoyable and to exploit any connections with other subjects. Where the story line is affected, make sure that students know what has happened, e.g.: summarise it yourself, or let a more able student read the story and tell the rest, or provide students with a written or taped translation.

A suggested list of omissions, indicated by ** in the commentaries, is as follows:

Stage 29  Masada II
Stage 30  polyspaston II
Stage 31  salūtātiō I
Stage 32  Euphrosynē revocāta I
Stage 33  in aulā Domitiānī II
Stage 34  exitium I

## 5 Preparation for GCSE

*Planning.* Most students who follow the Course from Book IV onwards will be working towards GCSE. At the start of Book IV, develop a plan for teaching Books IV and V and the GCSE syllabus. (If you have a generous time allowance, you may be able to include some of the material in Unit IVB (second and integrated editions) as preparation for the GCSE prescribed texts.) Factors influencing your selection of material include the needs and abilities of students, the teaching time and resources available, and the ultimate goals and interests of students. The plan provides a tool for evaluating progress and motivating students, and can be modified in the light of experience.

*Some ground rules* are useful. While your task is to set the pace, teach, assess and help, the job of preparing for the examination is the students'. They will need to:

a   make full use of time allocated to homework or private study;
b   know which tasks may be shared and which should be undertaken independently;
c   undertake a range of tasks including: preparation of new reading material and follow-up work like translation and comprehension; language revision exercises; note-writing and keeping folders; occasional timed assessment tasks;
d   accept some open-ended tasks without 'right answers' or follow-up;
e   record things that puzzle them so that they can seek help from you at the right time in an effective way.

*Unprepared passages*, comprehension or translation, should be introduced from the beginning of Book IV, with the incidence gradually increasing until they tackle one each week in the last six months before the examination. Students might start with passages from earlier Stages which you have omitted, advancing to more difficult passages. Give them a list of the unfamiliar vocabulary and ensure that the work is generally done in class where you are able to control conditions and timing.

*Prescribed texts* may have to be introduced at the end of Book IV or during the study of Book V. Students should approach them in the same way as the rest of their reading material. They will need to compile folders containing translations, previously agreed in class, together with notes arising from class discussion about language features, background and the author's style. If they are studying Roman life topics for the examination, they should likewise make new folders (or expand existing ones) with relevant notes, essays and illustrative materials. Make use of the examination boards' websites: AQA: www.aqa.org.uk; OCR: www.ocr.org.uk; SQA: www.sqa.org.uk.

*Practice in examination technique* enhances performance. From Book IV onwards, plan occasions when students tackle a test assignment for the appropriate length of time on their own. This builds up their confidence and enables you to give relevant individual advice on matters such as timing, reading questions carefully and answering what is asked, seeking for clues, referring to the text and selecting the best examples, and presenting work clearly.

## 6 Diverse teaching groups

Most of the students taking their study of Latin to Book IV and beyond will have chosen to do so, and they will have diverse goals and expectations. In selecting material consider their interests, allowing a choice where possible. For those who will not continue beyond GCSE, you will want to provide a memorable final experience. Latin literature offers enjoyment which can be prolonged by reading texts in translation, ideas which can challenge and stimulate, and a cultural experience which can widen and deepen the perspective which students bring to their other subjects and to their developing view of the world. Some may be motivated by their experience of their Latin course to take Classical Civilisation at AS, A2 or degree level.

Students benefit from some work in smaller groups of similar proficiency. While 'core' students might concentrate on translating a straightforward passage, potential AS and A2 Latin students might read a story omitted from your schedule, or tackle a passage in Unit IVB with the aid of a good translation, or undertake more detailed linguistic analysis of a passage.

## 7 Making the best use of teacher time

*Motivation.* The time you spend with students is the only opportunity you have to motivate them, apart from your written comments on their work. As the level of difficulty escalates, it is increasingly important for your contact with them to be enjoyable, varied, and confidence-building.

*Independent work.* Students can achieve a great deal on their own; one obvious example, already mentioned, is the compilation of literature and topic folders. Even more can be achieved by students working together in pairs or groups, especially if you develop in them from the outset habits of mutual criticism and support rather than dependency. They can unravel tricky passages, compare their findings, discuss points of style and character, and generally learn from each other. If possible, set aside a regular, guaranteed time for them to raise questions with you and receive personal advice.

*Resources.* Build up a stock of loan materials such as: audio cassettes or answer cards of correct exercises or translations; folders containing good student work built up over time; slide sets; digital material from the Cambridge Online Latin Project.

*Resource-based learning* is a well-attested technique, useful with heterogeneous groups or minimal time allocation. The characteristics are: it is student-centred; progress is matched against an agreed plan; pre-planned resources provide what is needed for the attempting and checking of learning tasks; the teacher is seen as a special 'resource' to provide periodic assessment, advice, and targets. A case study of resource-based learning is available from the Cambridge School Classics Project (www.cambridgescp.com).

## STAGE 29 Rōma

| Cultural background | Story line | Main language features | Focus of exercises |
|---|---|---|---|
| The Forum Romanum, heart of Rome and the empire.<br><br>The dedication of the arch of Titus, commemorating the conquest of Judaea. | Haterius, a wealthy contractor, and his workmen complete the arch of Titus, and the Jewish prisoners lament their fate. The mother of one of the prisoners, Simon, tells her son about the Roman sack of Jerusalem, the Jews' last stand at Masada, and his father's death in the mass suicide there. At the dedication of the arch next day, Simon seizes the sacrificial knife and kills his family and himself. | • Present and imperfect passive (3rd person singular and plural).<br><br>• Purpose clauses introduced by **quī** and **ubi**.<br><br>*Word patterns*<br>Compound verbs with **dē-, ex-** and **re-**. | 1 Imperfect subjunctive.<br><br>2 Agreement of present participles.<br><br>3 Selection of correct Latin words to translate an English sentence. |

## Opening page (p. 1)

**Illustration**. This model, made for Mussolini, shows Rome in the time of Constantine, 4th century AD, with a population of a million (*Museo della Civiltà Romana, Rome*). Ask students for their first impressions of the city. They may comment on its unplanned layout, its position on the Tiber and prominent buildings like the Colosseum and the Circus.

As preparation for the model sentences identify the Capitol, surmounted by the temple of Jupiter, and the Forum Romanum below. The annotated drawing on p. 43 will prove useful in pin-pointing these sites on the model.

This is probably sufficient by way of introduction to this Stage which concentrates on the Forum Romanum. Additional information on the city as a whole is given in the background section of Stage 31 and in the notes on the plan on p. 43 (see p. 40 of this Guide).

## Model sentences (pp. 2-3)

**Story**. A description of the Forum Romanum (notes on line drawings, below).

**New language feature**. Present passive, 3rd person singular and plural.

**New vocabulary**. appellātur, lectīcīs, ignis, Virginibus, extrēmō.

**First reading**. Build up a cumulative picture of the Forum by reading all the sentences through in Latin slowly enough for students to register each line drawing before you move on. Then elicit the correct translation by comprehension questions formulated in the passive, e.g. What is in the middle of Rome? What is it called?

Who is worshipped in the temple? What is the Forum filled with? What is heard there? etc. In discussing the drawing focus initially on the features described in the sentences and do not go into details unless students ask. (See notes below.)

**Discussion**. Ask students to write a translation of the model sentences, working in pairs. As you go over these, invite comment on the form of the Latin, and confirm that the **-ur** ending indicates a new form of the verb.

Encourage students to translate, using English passives for the time being, e.g. *is called, is worshipped, are greeted, are carried*, etc. As usual, students will be guided towards more flexibility in translation after some experience.

Concentrate on developing confidence in recognition and translation. English does not use the passive form as frequently, or as naturally, as Latin. In the course of language development, children begin to generate passive forms only at about thirteen years of age. Unless students themselves recognise the new verb-ending as passive, postpone terminology and explanation until 'About the language' (p. 8).

**Consolidation**. At the beginning or end of subsequent lessons, write up (or reproduce by OHP or data projector) for translation simple sentences in the passive form, based on the model sentences, e.g.:

negōtium in forō agitur.
pompae per forum dūcuntur.
ōrātiōnēs in forō audiuntur.
templum ā Virginibus Vestālibus cūrātur.
captīvī in carcere custōdiuntur.

or on the stories which follow, e.g.:

marmoris massae ad summum arcum tolluntur.
victimae ad sacrificium dūcuntur.

**Line drawings**: The drawings are reconstructions of today's ruins and depict Rome in the fourth century; they include some developments which took place after the time of the story.

1 *Capitol overlooking Forum*. On hilltop, temple of Jupiter Optimus Maximus, Juno and Minerva, centre of traditional Roman state religion. Next level, the Tarpeian rock, place of execution (left); **tabulārium**, the state record office (right). At Forum level, temple of Saturn, containing treasury (left); temple of Vespasian and Titus, probably unfinished at the time of the story (centre); temple of Concord (right). In the foreground: Basilica Julia, containing several law courts (left); Rostra (centre). The row of honorific columns in front of the Basilica Julia is fourth century.

2 *Close-up of Capitol and Forum*, showing a person of status being carried in a litter by eight bearers.

3 *Sacrificial procession*, with trumpeters leading the way, priest with head covered, carrying an axe, and ox garlanded for the sacrifice.

4 *Temple of Vesta*, containing the hearth fire of Rome which must never be allowed to go out. Smoke rises from the sacred fire which stands in the centre of the temple instead of the more usual statue. At an annual ceremony on March 1st, the flames were extinguished and then relit by concentrating the rays of the sun through a glass vessel of water.

**5** *The Rostra*, platform for political speeches, adorned along the front with the beaks (**rōstra**) of ships captured in war at the battle of Antium in 338 BC.

**6** *The prison.* Situated north of the Rostra (see plan, p. 16), it was on two levels. Cells on the upper level, of which only one now remains, housed criminals and suspects; on the lower level was the death cell (see photograph, p. 18 top, and note, p. 25 of this Guide).

Follow up this initial discussion by reading the background material, pp. 16-19. Aim at consolidating the information in the model sentences and at giving students a clear picture of the layout of the Forum. For example, provide them with an enlarged copy of the plan on p. 16 and ask them to annotate it with brief descriptions of the buildings they met in the model sentences. Students may be interested to see how much (or how little) remains of these buildings today in the photograph on pp. 16-17. There will be further opportunities to return to the background section later in the Stage.

## nox I (p. 4)

**Story**. A moonlit night in Rome finds rich men banqueting, poor men writing begging letters to their patrons or plotting crimes, and workmen desperately trying to complete the arch of Titus which is to be dedicated the next day.

**First reading**. The model sentences have given a taste of Rome by day; this passage presents Rome by night. Handle it briskly in a single lesson, so that the atmosphere of city life is firmly established, and the scene is set for **nox II**.

Start with an expressive Latin reading of the first paragraph, giving students a few moments to translate it in pairs, before you go over it. In discussing **nūlla quiēs, nūllum silentium,** compare the lack of peace and quiet in Rome with night time in London, or any familiar big city, and ask what would be disturbing the peace. Encourage students to think about the night life of the wealthy, and the darkness as cover for desperation or criminal activities.

Then read the next two paragraphs aloud in Latin. On the board create two columns headed **magnīs in domibus** and **in altīs īnsulīs**, and invite the class to explore the two paragraphs and suggest the points to be listed under each heading. Translation of the paragraphs could be set for homework. Going over the translations just before you read **nox II** will help students to recapture the night-time atmosphere.

Lines 13-23 are challenging, with imperfect actives and passives, new vocabulary and a difficult last sentence. One approach is to direct students' attention to the drawing on p. 5 and ask 'What signs are there in the picture that the arch is unfinished?' Elicit the points made in the 'Illustration' note on p. 16 of this Guide, linking discussion with relevant words in the glossary. Then use comprehension questions to elicit the meaning, e.g.:

Why was a great noise heard near the forum?
Where was the huge crane?
What three tasks were the workmen engaged in?
Why were they all working so hard?
What was the Emperor Domitian planning to do the next day?

What had he felt about his brother while Titus was alive?

Why had he decided to honour him now? Whose favour did he want to win?

What had been their attitude to Titus?

Translate these lines orally and follow up by a written translation of lines 19 (**nam Imperātor**)-23.

## Discussion

1 *Domitian's position.* Vespasian, Domitian's father, was commander of the Second Legion which invaded the south-west of Britain in AD 43 (Book II, pp. 56-7). He was entrusted by Nero with the task of quelling the Jewish revolt, and when he left Judaea for Rome to become emperor, his elder son, Titus, took over. Titus completed the defeat of the Jews, and succeeded his father as emperor in AD 79. When Domitian succeeded Titus in AD 81, he put up the arch to gain credibility with the people by associating himself with his father's and brother's success and popularity.

2 *Style.* Use questions to draw attention to stylistic features, e.g.:

In paragraph 2, which words does the writer use to convey a sense of luxury?

In paragraph 3, which words suggest poverty?

In lines 16-18, what is the effect of **aliī ... aliī ... aliī**?

In lines 20-21, which two words emphasise the change which had affected Domitian's attitude to his brother?

## Consolidation

Practise passive forms to develop confidence in recognition and translation, using simplified sentences from the story. It is helpful at this early stage to include the agent of the action, e.g.:

cēnae splendidae ā dīvitibus cōnsūmēbantur.

cibus ā servīs offerēbātur.

vīnum ab ancillīs fundēbātur.

carmina ā citharoedīs cantābantur.

magnus strepitus ā fabrīs tollēbātur.

arcus magnificus ā fabrīs exstruēbātur.

Revise the forms of the 4th declension by building up from paragraph 4 the pattern of the noun **arcus**:

**arcus** (nom) line 13, **arcuī** (dat.) line 14, **arcum** (acc.) line 15, **arcū** (abl.) line 16, **arcūs** (gen.) and **arcum** (acc.) line 17, **arcum** (acc.) lines 18 and 19. Study the declension on p. 114 and point out the difficult **-ūs** ending. Give practice with the following examples:

manūs puerī erant sordidae.

sacerdōs manūs ad caelum sustulit.

captīvus ad genua mīlitis sē iēcit.

supplex in genibus prō ārā manet.

cīvēs sonitūs audīvērunt.

gemmae ē manū fūris dēcidērunt.

For planning a revision programme for this Book see pp. 7-9.

## nox II (pp. 4-5)

**Story**. Under pressure from Salvius, Haterius drives his workmen to finish the arch before dawn. As silence falls, the cries of two women prisoners are heard.

**First reading**. Read lines 1-12 in Latin and help them to explore the meaning with questions, e.g.:

> Who was Q. Haterius Latronianus? What was he doing at the building site? How can you tell that he was anxious?
>
> What was Salvius doing there? Why was *he* anxious?
>
> How did he show his anxiety?
>
> What did the foreman try to do?
>
> What did he say? What examples does he give to indicate that the arch is on the very verge of completion? How does he give emphasis to his message?

If students have difficulty with the complex sentence **hic ... dēsisterent** (lines 5-7), it may be helpful to clarify its structure as follows:

> hic igitur fabrīs identidem imperāvit.
>
> hic igitur fabrīs identidem imperāvit nē labōre dēsisterent.
>
> hic igitur fabrīs, quamquam omnīnō fessī erant, identidem imperāvit nē labōre dēsisterent.

Lines 13-18 are straightforward enough for students to read on their own. The words of the lamentation (line 18), especially **Deus**, should be highlighted in preparation for the next story (see p. 17 of this Guide).

### Discussion topics

1   *Salvius' presence in Rome*. What are the implications of Salvius' presence in Rome as an adviser to Domitian? What does it suggest about his boast to Agricola (Book III p. 97) that he, rather than the general, knew the emperor's wishes? Was he acting under orders in plotting the murder of Cogidubnus (III, p. 11), in taking over Cogidubnus' palace and extorting money from the Britons (III, p. 126), and in murdering Belimicus (III, p. 131)? It is known that the historical Salvius was in Rome on 30th September, 81, in the early days of Domitian's principate, but the stories about him in Books II and III are fictitious. His career and relationship with the emperors are described in Book II (p. 21).

2   *Roman time*. The Romans divided every stretch of daylight and every stretch of darkness into twelve hours. Except at the equinox, daylight and night-time hours were of different lengths. Dawn broke at the first hour.

**Consolidation**. Ask students to write out a translation of Glitus' speech (lines 9-12). Use the instances of **arcus** for oral practice.

**Illustration**. The crane, partly shown on the left raising a stone block, will feature in the next Stage. On top of the arch the triumphal **quadrīga** (four-horse chariot) is only partly in place, and the winged Victory, playing a trumpet, still awaits her opposite number. Workmen holding torches provide light for others working on different parts of the arch. For the inscription, see p. 24 of this Guide.

## Masada I (pp. 6-7)

**Story**. The Jewish woman tells Simon, her eldest son, about Titus' sack of Jerusalem, the Jews' resistance to the Romans, and their final stand at Masada under Eleazar.

**First reading**. Read lines 1-11 aloud in Latin and then ask students to translate in pairs. As you go through their translation in class, check that they have given full weight to the range of tenses in this passage.

Read lines 12-19 in Latin, and follow with questions, e.g.:

What two questions did Simon ask? What did he beg his mother to do?

**sed tantus … dīcere posset** (lines 14-15). Why could Simon's mother not speak? What do you think was the cause of her grief?

Why had she not previously told her children about their father's death?

Why is she no longer afraid to tell the story?

Take lines 20-37 together so that the class appreciate the escalation and remorselessness of the Roman attack, and finish with a sense of climax and expectation. Refer the class to the photographs on pp. 6, 20 and 21, which illustrate the seemingly impregnable rock of Masada and the Roman siege works. Possible questions to use as you translate or to serve as a summary afterwards:

How long did the Jews rebel against the Romans (line 20)?

What terrible events occurred in the sack of Jerusalem (lines 22-5)?

How many Jews survived? What did they do (lines 26-7)?

How old was Simon at the time (lines 27-8)?

Look at the photograph on p. 6. Which Latin words describe it (lines 29-30)?

In which three ways did the Roman commander take action against the Jews (lines 31-5)? Was he confident of success or not? Give a reason for your answer.

### Discussion topics

1   *Jewish tradition*. Ask students to recall the words of the Jewish lament (p. 5, line 18). These words occur on several occasions in the Old Testament, and were used by Jesus on the Cross. Lamentation plays a traditional role in Jewish culture (cf. the famous chorus from Verdi's opera, *Nabucco*).

    The Temple in Jerusalem was, and still is, of central importance to the Jewish faith. After Titus' sack of Jerusalem all that was left was one wall of the foundation platform, which became known as the Wailing Wall, the holiest place in the world for Jews. The Dome of the Rock is a Muslim mosque built on top of this platform and is, after Mecca and Medina, the holiest place in the world for Muslims. This conjunction is one source of modern Jewish - Arab dispute. In line 24 note that **ipsum** is used to emphasise the speaker's veneration of the holy place, and her horror at the sacrilege perpetrated by the Romans.

    The sack of Jerusalem was a byword in the ancient world for dreadful devastation. Students should be able to cite modern parallels such as Dresden and Hiroshima.

2   Compare the woman's view of Titus (line 21) with that of the Roman people (p. 4, line 22).

## Consolidation

Elicit individual translations of lines 1-11. If students are still having difficulty with the long sentence **ūnā cum ... temptābat** (lines 5-6), use comprehension questions or build up the sentence gradually as suggested on p. 16 of this Guide.

Ask the class to identify the different ways in which the subjunctive is used in lines 12-19. If necessary, refer to p. 138.

This is a useful passage for revising the ablative case. Ask students in pairs to jot down all the examples of the ablative case they can find in lines 20-37, and how they would translate **duce Eleazārō** (line 26); **illō tempore** (line 27); **mūnītiōnibus** (line 30); **castellīs multīs** (line 32); **iussū** (line 32); **ignī** (line 35; do not labour this unfamiliar form). Compare translations, drawing up a list of all acceptable variants to consolidate the range of meanings.

Help students to identify the 4th declension nouns in this story, translate them in context and identify the case: **anus septuāgintā annōrum** (line 4), **nātū maximus** (line 6), **prope lacum** (line 29), **iussū Silvae** (line 32).

**Illustration**. The rock of Masada seen from the south, with the Dead Sea on the far right.

## ** Masada II (p. 7)

**Story**. Simon hears how most Jews, including his father, committed mass suicide rather than submit to the Romans, while his mother and grandmother hid underground with the children. He is inspired by his father's example.

**First reading**. Help the class with lines 1-6 and let them attempt the rest on their own. Check their understanding with comprehension questions.

## Discussion

1  **ego ipse mortem ... accipiō, servitūtem spernō** (lines 5-6). How does Eleazar emphasise the stark choice facing the Jews?
2  Did Simon's mother achieve anything by saving her children from the suicide pact?
3  Which words show most clearly Simon's opinion of what happened on Masada?
4  At the fall of Masada ten years ago, Simon was not quite five (**Masada I**, line 27). At fifteen he is now a young man. What do you think will happen?

## Consolidation

Ask the class to translate Eleazar's speech into an English version which will convey the charged atmosphere. Some students may be prepared to read their own versions aloud dramatically.

**Masada I** and **II** contain examples of the pronouns **ego, tū, nōs, vōs** and **sē**. Divide the class into two and set half to find the pronouns in **Masada I** (lines 10-37) and the other half to find those in **Masada II**. Tell them to be prepared to translate the sentence containing the pronoun and to state its case. With students' help build up tables on the board or reproduce the complete tables by OHP or data projector and tick off the cases found in the stories. There are further opportunities for pronoun practice on p. 120.

At this point read 'The Jews and the Romans' (pp. 19-20) so that students can set what they have just read in its wider context and be prepared for the next passage describing the dedication of the arch of Titus.

# About the language 1: passive verbs (p. 8)

**New language feature.** Present and imperfect passive, 3rd person singlar and plural.

**Discussion.** Read through paragraphs 1-3 with the class. They will already be familiar with the terms 'active' and 'passive' which they have met in connection with the participles. Ask them to describe the difference between the examples in paragraph 1 and those in paragraph 2. If they say 'They mean the same' accept this, but encourage them to work out for themselves that the action is the same, but seen from a different point of view. The following pairs of pictures and captions may help to make the point.

**active:** servī vīnum **fundēbant**.
*Slaves were pouring the wine.*

**passive:** vīnum ā servīs **fundēbātur**.
*The wine was being poured by slaves.*

**active:** puer versūs **legit**.
*The boy is reading verses.*

**passive:** versūs ā puerō **leguntur**.
*Verses are being read by the boy.*

Then set students to translate the examples in paragraph 4.

**Consolidation**. Ask students to write a translation of p. 7, lines 20-8, or to pick out and translate examples of the passive form of the verb on pp. 6-7. In several subsequent lessons give a few minutes to oral practice with further examples, e.g.:

> puer iānuam claudit. iānua ā puerō clauditur.
> nūntius spectāculum nūntiat. spectāculum ā nūntiō nūntiātur.
> pauperēs ad patrōnōs epistulās scrībēbant. epistulae ad patrōnōs ā pauperibus
> scrībēbantur.
> multī Rōmānī Masadam circumveniēbant. Masada ā multīs Rōmānīs
> circumveniēbātur.

A quick way of giving practice in handling the passive is to ask for English sentences to be turned from active to passive and vice versa.

## arcus Titī I (p. 9)

**Story**. Salvius and Haterius are among the crowd which gathers next morning to watch the procession of musicians, sacrificial bulls, Jewish treasure, Jewish prisoners, emperor, consuls and statue of Titus.

**First reading**. This is an opportunity to let the class attempt a Latin passage unaided. Allocate 'The scene at the arch' (lines 1-14) to half the class, and 'The procession' (lines 15-30) to the other half, and ask students to draw or list all the components of their scene. Some may like to prepare a broadcast commentary. Then let each group give descriptions of the scene to the other.

**Discussion**. Read lines 1-14 aloud and examine the content in more depth by asking questions, e.g.:

> Where do senators sit (lines 6-7)? Which phrase suggests that many senators
> were insincere in their enthusiasm to witness the ceremony? What was in
> Salvius' mind as he chose his seat?
> How do the arrangements made for equites differ from those for senators
> (lines 9-10)? What does this tell you about their social status?
> What arrangements are being made to secure the approval of the gods
> (lines 12-14)? If necessary, remind students of the information about religious
> ritual in Book III, Stage 23.

Repeat the process with lines 15-30, e.g.:

> Why was the Jewish treasure put on display (lines 18-21)? Which elements of it
> can you recognise in the photograph of the carving on p. 10?
> What was the Roman attitude to prisoners? Are there modern parallels? How is
> the status of the emperor emphasised?
> Why was it suitable for Lucius Flavius Silva to be with the emperor on this
> occasion?

### Consolidation

Pick out examples of 5th declension nouns, identify their cases in context and then put them up in case order. Add further examples from pp. 6-7.

diēs festus (p. 9, line 2), nūlla spēs (p. 7, line 4);
effigiem Titī (p. 9, line 29), cum ... rem cōnfēcissent (p. 7, line 9);
eō diē (p. 9, line 3), spē favōris (p. 9, line 7);
in rēbus adversīs (p. 6, lines 7-8);

Revise the declension (p. 114), pointing out that all cases of **diēs** (except the nominative singular) have affinities with corresponding cases in other declensions, and give students more practice with examples in sentences, e.g.:

tandem diēs festus adest!
diem festum Rōmānī celebrant.
illō diē omnēs ad arcum convēnērunt..
captīvī omnem spem āmīserant.
multōs diēs captīvī in carcere mānsērunt.
rem dīram māter timēbat.
spē favōris multī senātōrēs aderant.
Simōn in rēbus adversīs fortitūdinem praestitit.

Remind students of 4th declension nouns: **ad arcum** (line 1), **iussū** (line 4), **prō arcū** (line 12), **serēnō vultū** (lines 23-4), **currū magnificō** (line 27), **magistrātūs nōbilissimī** (line 29).

Give oral practice with passive verbs, e.g. by following up **pompa dūcēbātur** (lines 4-5) with **pompae dūcēbantur** and **pompa dūcitur** and so on.

This would be a good time to trace the processional route through the Forum to the arch of Titus, with the help of the plan and illustrations on pp. 16-18 and the information about the Via Sacra on p. 18.

## arcus Titī II (pp. 10-11)

**Story**. After congratulating Salvius and sending thanks to Haterius, Domitian dedicates the arch. Simon seizes the sacrificial knife and kills his family and himself.

**First reading**. Divide the story into manageable sections with titles, e.g.:
*The arrival.* **ad arcum ... ageret** (lines 1-5), questions 1-5.
*The ceremony.* **inde ad āram ... aguntur** (lines 5-9), questions 6-8.
*The interruption.* **subitō ... pedem rettulit** (lines 10-13), questions 9-12.
*Simon's defiance.* **nōn Imperātōrem ... trānsfīxit** (lines 13-21), questions 13-15.

Read each section in Latin twice. Between the two readings ask students to study the questions for that section; remind them to find clues to the meaning in the questions. After the second reading give them time to study the Latin and answer the questions. If you move around as they work at their answers, you will be able to identify anything which is causing difficulty and either help immediately or plan further practice at a later time. The class may need considerable help with question 15. It is useful to take in the answers for marking, and return in a later lesson to do more work on the story. This is a good routine to establish with straightforward narratives as preparation for GCSE. The answers and mark scheme are as follows:

|   |   | Marks |
|---|---|---|
| 1 | Domitian's purpose was to make a sacrifice. | 1 |
| 2 | He greeted the senators and equites. | 1 |
| 3 | (The sight of) the arch. He summoned Salvius and praised him highly | 1 + 2 |
| 4 | He ordered Salvius to thank Haterius. | 1 |
| 5 | He may not have wanted to meet someone of a lower social class *or similar*. | 1 |
| 6 | The victim was to have its throat cut (with a knife). *Accept 'A slave presented the victim's throat to the emperor to be cut' or similar.* | 1 |
| 7 | The god Titus; the divine/deified/dead Titus. | 1 |
| 8 | The victim was being sacrificed to Titus, the arch was being dedicated to him; the (greatest) thanks were being expressed to him by the Roman people. *Accept direct speech. If active forms of the verb are used then the other relationships within the sentence should be correctly expressed.* | 3 |
| 9 | The Romans were concentrating on the sacrifice. | 1 |
| 10 | He wanted to seize the knife. | 1 |
| 11 | **audāciā eius attonitī/immōtī stābant.** | 1 |
| 12 | He feared assassination *or similar*. | 1 |
| 13 | Simon embraced his mother and grandmother and immediately killed them (with the knife). | 2 |
|  | Then he killed his brothers (who did not resist at all), in the same way. | 1 |
| 14 | Simon cursed the Roman people (in a loud voice) and stabbed himself (with the knife). | 2 |
| 15 | Like Eleazarus, Simon said the Jews preferred to die rather than be slaves of the Romans. | 2 |
|  | He killed himself after killing his family just as Eleazarus brought about the death of his fellow Jews and then himself. | 2 |

TOTAL **25**

## Discussion topics

1 *The arch.* Do you agree with Domitian's admiration of the workmanship of the arch (illustrations pp. 10, 15 and 24)? How do we know that it celebrated a victory over the Jews? What is depicted in the carving? How would a Jew regard the carving?

    What was Domitian's motive in setting up the arch? Why do you think he had it placed at the entrance to the ancient Forum Romanum (see illustration p. 18), rather than in one of the more modern fora?

2 *Simon's behaviour.* Can you understand why Simon did what he did? Do you think he was right? (Note: the details about the fate of the Jewish prisoners in this Stage are fictitious.) Would people act like this today?

## Consolidation

Pick out participial phrases and ask the class to identify who is described by the participle and which case is used: **ē currū ēgressus** (line 1), **admīrātiōne affectus** (line 3), **ad sē arcessītum** (line 4), **ad āram prōgressus** (line 5), **haec locūtus** (line 7), **occāsiōnem nactus** (line 11), **audāciā eius attonitī** (lines 12-13), **pavōre commōtus** (line 13), **in manū tenēns** (line 14), **haec locūtus** (line 18), **mātrem ... amplexus** (lines 18-19), **haudquāquam resistentēs** (lines 19-20), **populum ... dētestātus** (line 21). Note in particular how students cope with the examples where the participle and the noun in agreement occur in different sentences.

Further practice of present participles is provided by exercise 2, p. 14.

**Illustration.** Detail of carving inside the arch. The Jewish treasure from the Temple in Jerusalem is shown being carried in Titus' triumph, which had taken place after the sack of Jerusalem. The items visible are (from left to right): a placard naming the object being carried nearby; the menorah (the sacred candlestick with seven branches), supported at shoulder level on poles; another placard; the golden table from the temple, with the next placard to the right, and the silver trumpets in front. On the right is a triumphal arch through which the procession is passing.

## About the language 2: more about purpose clauses (p. 12)

**New language feature.** Purpose clauses introduced by the relative pronoun and conjunctions other than **ut**. The examples given are introduced by **quī** and **ubi**.

**Discussion.** Help students to recognise that the old man in example 1, and the woman in example 2, both acted with an *intention,* or purpose; the sentences do not indicate whether the intention was actually carried out. The subjunctive form of the verb is used to show this. Compare the sentence in paragraph 2 with: **fēmina servum mīsit quī cibum ēmit**.

We use several different English expressions to express purpose. Generate as many different ways as possible of translating the examples in paragraph 3.

**Consolidation.** See if students can identify those sentences on pp. 9 and 10 which express intention or purpose (either with **ut** or some other introductory word. Half the class could take p. 9 and half p. 10). The sentences are.:

inter eōs ... esset (p. 9, lines 7-9).
aderant ... īnspicerent (p. 9, lines 13-14).
Domitiānus ... faceret ... salūtāvit (p. 10, lines 1-2).
inde ... sacrificāret (p. 10, lines 5-6).

Do not draw attention to **nē ... perīrētis** (p. 6, lines 16-17), unless a student recognises it as a purpose. If this happens, confirm that it is an *intention to prevent other people from doing something*, and ask them to look out for more examples in the coming stories.

Practise recognition of the subjunctive by setting sentences in pairs for translation, basing them on paragraph 3, e.g.:

sacerdōs haruspicem arcessīvit quī victimam īnspexit.
sacerdōs haruspicem arcessīvit quī victimam īnspiceret.

Haterius quīnque fabrōs ēlēgit quī figūrās in arcū sculperent.
Haterius quīnque fabrōs ēlēgit quī figūrās in arcū sculpsērunt.

Ask students what part of the verb appears when the personal endings are subtracted from the imperfect subjunctive (see p. 128).

This may be a suitable moment at which to take exercise 1, p. 14.

**Illustration**. Statue of Titus (*British Museum*). Do you think he shows any family likeness to Domitian (p. 110)?

## Word patterns: compound verbs 1 (p. 13)

**New language feature**. Verbs formed with the prefixes **dē-**, **ex-** and **re-**.

**Discussion**. Ask students to work through the page for homework and go over their work in a subsequent lesson. The study of English derivatives in paragraph 5 may be extended by using examples from paragraphs 1-3.

## Practising the language (pp. 14-15)

*Exercise 1*. Complete the sentences with the imperfect subjunctive by adding the appropriate personal endings to the given infinitives. Less able students may need help with this exercise.

*Exercise 2*. Complete the sentences by selecting the correct participle from the alternatives provided.

*Exercise 3*. Translate English sentences into Latin by selecting from the alternative Latin words provided. Explain your choice.

**Illustration**. The arch of Titus today (note standing figure at left for scale). Ask students to compare this photograph with the line drawing on p. 24 and to identify what is missing. Note the decorative features: two winged victories filling in the triangular spaces immediately above the curve of the arch, and a triumphal procession in the shade of the overhang just above them. The inscription reads as follows (brackets represent explanatory additions):

| | |
|---|---|
| SENATVS | *The Senate* |
| POPVLVSQVE ROMANVS | *and the Roman people (give this arch)* |
| DIVO TITO DIVI VESPASIANI F(ILIO) | *to the Divine Titus, Divine Vespasian's son,* |
| VESPASIANO AVGVSTO | *Vespasian Augustus* |

DIVO (*divine*) is the title given to a dead emperor who has been deified.

## Cultural background material (pp. 16-21)

**Content**. There are three topics in the cultural background of this Stage:
- the Roman Forum (best introduced with the model sentences and studied in more detail at appropriate points in the Stage);
- the arch of Titus (see **nox** I and **II**, pp. 4-5, and **arcus Titī** I and **II**, pp. 9-10); other public monuments and buildings;
- the conquest of Judaea by the Romans, which forms the background to the story told to Simon in **Masada** I and **II**, pp. 6-7.

## Discussion

1   *Scene in the Forum Romanum.* Encourage students to identify the major buildings illustrated on pp. 16-17. Let them use their recollections of Pompeii and the provinces to fill out their mental picture of the scene in the Roman Forum, and describe the activities which would occur there. What would have been the reaction of a British or an Egyptian visitor to the scene in the Roman Forum?

2   *Monumental architecture in the centre of Rome.* What was the purpose of the arch of Titus? How did its architecture contribute to this? Examine the pictures of different Roman public buildings in the Forum. What decoration did they have? Which features, or which buildings, do you consider to be characteristically Roman? Which features of Roman architecture do you see in many towns or cities today?

3   *The Romans and the Jews.* Why did the Jews find Roman rule intolerable? Why were the Jews able to harass the Romans so effectively and hold out against them for so long? What happened to the Jewish nation as a result of this utter defeat by the Romans?

## Illustrations

pp. 16-17

- Three views of the Roman Forum. Plan and photograph are both seen from the Palatine; the reconstruction looks towards the Palatine, from point 7 on the plan. The brick senate-house (8) had a marble portico in front but above the line of vision was, like so many Roman buildings, coated in stucco to imitate marble. The nearby arch of Septimius Severus would not have been there at the time of the stories in this Stage. The lower part of the darker stone building (top left of photograph) is what remains of the Tabularium, the public record office. The imperial fora are underneath and beyond the trees (top right).

p.18

- Inside the prison. This circular Etruscan water cistern, with a hole in the roof for lowering a bucket, became the Roman death cell, and was described by the Roman historian, Sallust, writing in 40 BC, as 'repugnant and fearsome from neglect, darkness and stench'. It was the place where convicted enemies of the state were strangled, if they were not publicly thrown off the Tarpeian rock. It is now a Christian chapel because it was the place of imprisonment of Saints Peter and Paul.

- A reconstructed fragment of the temple of Vesta, with the house of the Vestal Virgins in the background. They held a privileged position in Roman society, enjoying, for instance, front seats at the games, but any infringement of their virginity was punishable by being immured alive. There were six vestals, selected at the age of 6-10 from noble families, who served for thirty years and were then free to return to private life, even to marry, although few were willing to sacrifice their status for the subordinate role of a Roman wife.

- The Sacred Way, paved with hard volcanic stone, winding up to the arch of Titus which is here seen from the Forum, the opposite direction from earlier illustrations. The inscription on this side is modern, recording those who reconstructed the arch in 1822, using travertine stone to distinguish it from the original work in Pentelic marble.

p. 19 • Remains of a synagogue on the rock of Masada. Built as palace stables by Herod the Great, it was later turned into a synagogue for 250 people, by the addition of tiers of benches.

• Baths at Masada, with floor raised over hypocaust, and flues in walls, showing that the Jewish palace enjoyed the luxuries of the Roman world.

p. 20 • Drawing of pottery sherd bearing Eleazar's name, possibly used for drawing lots.

• The view from Masada looking down at the camp which was Silva's head-quarters. One of a ring of eight, it has the typical shape of a Roman camp. Note the curving protective barrier at the entrance, and the inner camp.

p. 21 • General view of Masada from the air.

p. 22 • Reverse of a coin of Vespasian, celebrating Titus' defeat of the Jews. A bronze sestertius, it was minted by decree of the Senate (**SC - senātūs cōnsultō**). At this time the Senate minted bronze and copper coins, while the emperor had the monopoly of minting gold and silver coins.

## Checklist vocabulary: cognates and compounds

audāx, audēre, dēscendere, revenīre, scelestus, vīta.
(See the Introduction to this Guide, p. 9.)

## Suggested activities

1  You are a Roman citizen at the dedication of the arch of Titus, standing next to an Egyptian visitor, who had experience of riots against the Jews in Alexandria. Explain what is going on and what it means.

2  You are a Jewish general. You led resistance against the Romans. When your city fell, part way through the war, Titus treated you well and you now live in Rome as a friend of the imperial family. Although you are still a Jew by faith, you have changed your name from Joseph ben Matthias to Flavius Josephus. You plan to write a book about the Jewish War. Draw up a summary for your book, using the information on pp. 19-21 to explain: why the Jews rebelled, what the Roman army did when Jerusalem fell, what you felt when you were captured, how you found out about the end of the war at Masada, and your feelings about your own change of fortune and the dedication of the arch. When you have finished your summary, read Josephus' story of his capture in *The Jewish War* trans. G. Williamson (Penguin Classics, pp. 220-2).

3  Make an annotated plan of the Forum (as suggested on p. 14 of this Guide). Include it in a folder (to be developed during Stages 30 and 31) about important buildings in Rome in the 1st century AD. Make notes about materials and methods of construction, where the buildings stood in the city, what they were used for, and what effect they might have had on the citizens.

Students will find *The Ancient City* by Peter Connolly and Hazel Dodge is very helpful.

# STAGE 30 Haterius

| Cultural background | Story line | Main language features | Focus of exercises |
|---|---|---|---|
| Roman building techniques. | While Salvius basks in the emperor's approval, Haterius waits angrily for the promised reward of a priesthood. Taking Salvius aloft in his crane, he demands satisfaction. Salvius sells him a well-placed burial plot. Dazzled by the vision of a grand and enduring memorial, Haterius fails to pursue the question of the priesthood. | • Perfect passive.<br><br>• Pluperfect passive.<br><br>**Word patterns**<br>Nouns ending in -tās and related adjectives. | 1 Present and imperfect active and passive.<br><br>2 Agreement of perfect passive participles.<br><br>3 Pluperfect subjunctive. |

## Opening page (p. 23)

**Illustration**. Carving from the monument of the Haterii, a very elaborate tomb three miles outside Rome on the Via Labicana (*Vatican Museum*). An example of popular art, ornate and elaborate in detail, with characteristic out-of-scale figures, in contrast with the restrained elegance and stylised realism of official monuments.

The carving shows a mausoleum being built with the aid of a crane and, crammed in above, the lying-in-state of a dead person, with a bent old woman sacrificing before a flaming altar. The mausoleum is decorated with portraits of some of the people to be buried inside. The crane (explained on p. 35) was probably worked by an experienced gang of free workmen, since it required steady and skilled operation. The mausoleum is shown completed, and men have climbed the steps running up the jib of the crane and attached a spray of greenery to symbolise the end of building work (Jean-Pierre Adam in *Roman building*). Visible are: two men on the ground holding ropes to brake the crane; lifting ropes, which go down behind the wheel, so that any load is out of sight; vegetation being tied on with a reef knot; the ropes to the pulleys which are supporting guys for the crane, to rock it back and forth, not for lifting.

Tombs often show a door ajar into the next world (bottom right). Behind the balustrade (bottom left) is a dome-shaped altar like that pictured on a saucepan handle in Bath (Book III, p. 1).

The tomb of the Haterii also shows carvings of the Colosseum, the arch of Titus and another triumphal arch. This, with the carving of the crane, suggests that at least one of the Haterii was a builder and involved in the construction of prestigious monuments.

### Illustration

p. 24 An impressionistic drawing of the completed arch showing the interior. Note the coffered ceiling and the carving in the centre, which shows Titus being borne to heaven on the back of an eagle; the carvings of the triumphal procession (see p. 10) inside the archway; the figures which probably stood on the top of the completed arch; and the view of buildings beyond the arch, looking towards the Forum. The drawing sets the scene for the model sentences and for the first story, **dignitās**, from which the caption (bottom of p. 24) is taken.

## Model sentences (p. 25)

**Story**. After the dedication, crowds gather to admire the arch of Titus. Haterius looks forward to the reward promised him by Salvius but, as time passes, begins to worry that he has been deceived.

**New language feature**. Perfect passive, 3rd person singular (masculine and neuter), with one 1st person example. 3rd person plural forms are introduced in the following story.

**First reading**. After a lively Latin reading, the model sentences on p. 25 are easy to understand in the light of the Stage 29 stories and Salvius' character.

**Discussion**. Producing a correct translation of the new forms is more challenging. Use the adverbs of time **heri, nūper, adhūc** ('What happened yesterday?' etc.) to guide students to a correct translation (*was dedicated ... was promised ... was praised ... has been sent, have been deceived*).

Do not comment on the verb forms unless students query the translation of **est** by a past tense. If they do, confirm that it is acceptable to translate **dēdicātus est** by *was dedicated,* and **missum est** by *has been sent*. If they probe further, use the explanation given on p. 31 of this Guide.

**Consolidation**. Return to check the translation of the model sentences in several ways (writing, oral work, with books open, with books closed, etc.) as you proceed with reading the rest of the Stage.

## dignitās (pp. 26-7)

**Story**. Haterius' wife, Vitellia, discovers that he is furious because Salvius has not delivered the promised priesthood, a key to social advancement. She suggests taking Salvius up in the crane to impress him and jog his memory.

**First reading**. This is a challenging story, and needs careful handling if it is not to flag. One approach is to steer the class through the dialogue as quickly as possible, ensuring that they understand the argument before they tackle the questions. Take the passage in three parts:
*Situations of Salvius and Haterius, lines 1-13*. Your Latin reading will demonstrate the contrasting atmospheres. Divide the class into pairs and ask one student in each pair to study the first paragraph and the other the second. Establish by easy oral comprehension questions the feelings of the general public, Salvius and Haterius before setting the class to write down the answers to questions 1-7 on p. 27.
*Haterius' grievance, lines 14-43*. Steer the class through the dialogue briskly, but ensure that they understand the abstract theme. Each pair of speeches by Vitellia and Haterius make convenient sense units, i.e., lines 14-21, 22-6, 27-33, 34-43. Read each pair aloud, then establish the salient points by your own questions. Students will probably need help with the idea that Haterius is not content with counting his

blessings or amassing more wealth but is concerned only with social advancement and increased personal prestige. Modern comparisons will help to make the point. *Vitellia's plan, lines 44-8*. Students may find the last two sentences difficult linguistically, but the sense is straightforward.

After this preliminary treatment of the dialogue, students could tackle questions 8-15 for homework. Answers and mark scheme are as follows:

## Marks

|  |  |  |
|---|---|---|
| 1 | Four days. | 1 |
| 2 | Roman citizens kept on gathering/gathered at the arch (daily) to examine the figures sculpted on it/the reliefs. | 2 |
| 3 | To congratulate him. | 1 |
| 4 | The emperor had highly praised Haterius' arch. | 1 |
| 5 | They were not admitted. | 1 |
| 6 | **īrā commōtus** or **saeviēbat**. | 1 |
| 7 | Vitellia tried to soothe him. | 1 |
| 8 | Vitellia thought Haterius had been working too hard/was neglecting his health. | 1 |
| 9 | She suggested that he must rest. | 1 |
| 10 | A huge reward was promised to him by Salvius, but he had not received any reward, not even thanks. | 3 |
| 11 | **Two of**: He was a very famous contractor/his arch had been recently praised by the emperor (himself)/ he had erected many public buildings/(from these) he had gained great wealth. | 2 |
| 12 | Prestige/status *or similar*. | 1 |
| 13 | Vitellia's sister was Rufilla, the wife of Salvius, who had always favoured Haterius and often recommended him to the emperor. | 3 |
| 14 | A priesthood/he wanted to become a priest. | 1 |
|  | A consulship. | 1 |
| 15 | Vitellia suggested that Haterius should invite Salvius to his builder's yard and show off his crane to him. | 2 |
|  | While Salvius was overcome with admiration, Haterius should ask him about a priesthood. | 2 |

TOTAL **25**

## Discussion topics

1 Why should Salvius be so pleased that the emperor praised Haterius (line 6)?
2 Why is it that Salvius, rather than Haterius, appears to have got what he wanted from the building of the arch?
3 How is Haterius' mood in this story similar to that of Memor (Book III, p. 7), before Salvius arrives in Bath? How did Salvius treat Memor? Who gained more from the relationship? What is Haterius' long-term ambition? Why does he have

more influence over Salvius than Memor did?

Note: Haterius is a fictional character, suggested by the tomb of the Haterii. A rich and successful building contractor, he has improved his position by marrying a high-born wife whose sister is married to an up-and-coming political figure. Yet he is still disadvantaged by his modest origins in a minor branch of the Haterii, hence his desire for a priesthood. His cultivation of Salvius and his work on the arch have brought him the personal notice of the emperor, but not the permanent advancement he desires.

4   What does the title mean? To whom does it refer? Were Salvius and Haterius seeking different things, or were they both seeking the same thing?

5   What picture are we given of Vitellia? How does she compare with her sister, Rufilla? Note that she is more than a sympathetic wife. She is fully aware of the advantages that Haterius has gained by marrying into her aristocratic family. Her plan (lines 44-8) is not only novel and clever but also shows psychological insight: by getting Haterius to do something practical with his beloved crane, she jerks him out of his frustration and anger.

**Consolidation**

Ask students to prepare a brief passage for reading aloud in Latin, giving them a choice of atmospheric description (paragraphs 1 or 2), or characterisation (Haterius or Vitellia). Encourage them to ask for help if they are not sure of the meaning, and make a note of any difficulties for subsequent work.

This passage contains several irregular verbs: **posset** (line 10), **possum** (line 21), **(in)tulit** (line 22), **es** (line 27), **esse** (line 40) **volō** (line 39), **nōlī** (line 44). Ask students for the meaning of the example in the text and then, with the help of pp. 132-3, change one element of the verb at a time and ask for a translation of the form substituted, e.g. **es** means *you are*. What would be the meaning of **sumus? erāmus? erimus?** etc. After several short sessions of oral practice, students could revise the forms of these verbs for homework, concentrating on tense discrimination rather than the easier person discrimination.

With textbooks open at p. 118, consolidate comparatives and superlatives by using the examples in this passage: **plūrimī** (line 3), **nōtissimus** (line 27), **magnās** (line 29), **maximās** (line 32), **amplissima** (line 34), **dītissimus, nōbilissimā** (line 35), **optimum** (line 44), **maius, mīrābilius** (line 46). For example, ask students:

Which word would Vitellia have used if she had said 'You are a very rich
    contractor'?
Which words in the story mean 'great, greater, greatest'?
How would you translate **optimum** (line 44)?
Which words on p. 118 mean 'good' and 'better'?

In connection with the neuter forms in line 46, ask students to give you the English for examples which are already familiar to them, e.g. **melius est tibi testāmentum facere** (Book III, p.5); **melius est tibi hunc senātōrem vidēre** (Book III, p. 8); **melius est mihi ad culīnam īre** (Book III, p. 75).

Now turn to the table on p. 119 that sets out the declension of **longior** and **longissimus**, and look in particular at the neuter forms of **longior**. The comparison made in paragraph 4 with 3rd declension neuter nouns such as **tempus** may help to persuade students that the **-ius** ending is not a complete aberration. Follow up this session with further practice based on pp. 118-19. Students may need help with the examples in paragraph 5, p. 119.

Check that students are recognising and translating accurately examples of the perfect and pluperfect active before they study the forms and meanings of the passives.

## About the language 1: perfect passive tense (p. 28)

**New language feature**. The perfect passive tense is introduced by comparison with the perfect active. Students have so far met examples of the 3rd person singular and plural, and two examples of the 1st person; this note explains and completes the tense.

**Discussion**. Read through paragraph 1 with the class. Point out that, like the perfect active tense, the perfect passive has alternative English translations, and the context of a story will indicate which one to use.

Ask the class to study the complete tense in paragraph 2. They should be able to tell you the two parts that make up the tense before reading the explanation in paragraph 3. If they query the use of the present tense of **esse**, explain that it is the perfect participle that affects the translation. It may be helpful to give the literal translation of **portātus sum** *I am having been carried*, i.e. *I have been carried*.

The examples in paragraph 4 , which are all masculine singular or plural, give students an opportunity to concentrate on the singular and plural forms. Ask for both translations of the verb.

In handling paragraph 5, about gender agreement between verb and subject, it may be helpful to return to the verbs in model sentences 1 and 2 (**dēdicātus est, prōmissum est, laudātus est, missum est, dēceptus sum**), noticing how the participle agrees with **arcus, praemium** and **ego**.

**Consolidation**. Ask students to pick out as many examples as possible of the perfect passive tense from pp. 26-7 and ask for the appropriate translation: **arcus ... dēdicātus est** (line 1); **Salvius ... gaudiō affectus est** (line 5); **vōcēs audītae sunt** (lines 7-8); **amīcī admissī sunt** (line 8); **ego ... dēceptus sum** (lines 23-4); **praemium prōmissum est** (line 25); **arcus laudātus est** (line 28); **nihil ... factum est** (lines 46-7). In each case, ask students whether the participle is singular or plural.

## polyspaston I (p. 29)

**Story**. Haterius takes Salvius to see the crane, and offers him a view over the city. With the workmen looking on, Salvius cannot refuse, but keeps his eyes shut tight as the crane is hoisted.

**First reading**. Read the story in Latin, a paragraph at a time, checking students' understanding with questions as you go, e.g.:

When did Haterius take Salvius to his yard? What was his purpose?
What was the foreman doing? When he saw the boss approaching, how did his behaviour change? (lines 2-4)

**tōta ārea ... erat** (line 5). What does this sentence mean? Which word means noise? In which case is it?

Three things were going on in the yard. What were they (lines 5-7)?

Where did Haterius take Salvius to see the crane? How had it been prepared by the workmen? (lines 9-10)

What did Haterius say his crane could offer Salvius (lines 12-14)?

What made Salvius go pale? Why did he hide his fear? (lines 15-16)

How were Haterius and Salvius raised to the sky? What did Salvius do while this was happening? (lines 18-20)

**Discussion.** What do you think Vitellia expected to happen, when she suggested Haterius should show Salvius his crane? Do you think Haterius is in a strong position to secure the priesthood, now that he and Salvius are up in the air?

**Consolidation.** If students have had difficulty with the long sentence **sed ... cōnsēdit** (lines 15-17), the method of analysis suggested on p. 16 of this Guide may be helpful.

Set a written translation of lines 5-12: **tōta ārea ... polyspaston?**

Ask students to find one example each of:

  purpose clause: **ut ... ostentāret** (lines 1-2);
  present participle: **appropinquantem** (line 3), **labōrantium** (line 5), **dissimulāns** (line 16);
  perfect passive participle: **occupātōs** (line 8), **fīxam** (line 15), **dēfīxōs** (line 16), **cōnfectus, clausīs** (line 20);
  indirect command: **imperāvit ut ... traherent** (lines 18-19).

Have these translated in the context of the complete sentence. Note the absence of an agreeing noun or pronoun in the case of **labōrantium** (line 5).

Pick out nouns from the text and ask students for their meaning and case. In particular make sure that the forms of the ablatives are recognised in preparation for the introduction of the ablative absolute in the next Stage. Spend a few minutes every lesson on this activity to develop confidence in recognition and analysis. If it seems necessary, develop further work from selected examples drawn from pp. 114-15 and 135.

## ** polyspaston II (p. 30)

**Story.** Exclaiming at the view, Salvius spots the new arch and recalls the emperor's delight, provoking Haterius to demand the promised priesthood. Making the excuse that Domitian has not yet made up his mind, Salvius fobs him off with a burial plot.

**First reading.** Explore the passage through a lively Latin reading and comprehension questions. Let the subject matter determine the sections into which you divide the passage, e.g.:

*The view.* **Salvius ... fulget!** (lines 1-4).

  How does Salvius show his feelings when he opens his eyes? What can he see?
  Why does the arch stand out (lines 3-4)?

*The reward.* **Imperātor ... exspectō** (lines 4-12).

  What two things happened when the emperor saw the arch (lines 4-6)?
  What does Haterius say pleases him greatly (lines 7-8)?

**sed** (line 8). What does this word suggest he is going to say next?

Translate **praemium ... accēpī** (lines 8-9). If you were reading this sentence aloud, which word(s) would you emphasise?

What does Salvius say about the priesthood (lines 10-12)? Do you believe him? Why?

*The burial plot.* **aliquid ... trādere possum** (lines 12-20).

**aliquid ... possum** (line 12). What does **intereā** mean? Why is it an important word in the sentence?

What does Salvius own (line 13)? Where is it situated (lines 13-14)? What does Salvius suggest to Haterius (lines 14-15)?

Why does he mention the Metelli and the Scipiones?

How does Haterius feel when he hears the offer (line 16)? Would you expect him to be quite so pleased at having to buy his reward?

What does he envisage building on the plot of land (lines 17-19)? For whom? How will it be decorated?

In what way will this satisfy his need for status (lines 19-20)? Why does this speech put Haterius in a weak bargaining position?

*The deal.* **prō agellō ... contentus** (lines 20-9).

What sum does Haterius offer (line 21)?

Why does Salvius smile (line 22)? Would he let Haterius see him smile?

What comment does he make about the sum (line 23)? Why might this be true?

What reason does Salvius give for doing Haterius a favour (lines 23-4)?

What is the sum finally agreed (line 24)?

What order did Haterius give to the workmen (line 27)?

Which of the phrases, **alter spē ... pecūniā contentus** (lines 28-9), applies to Haterius and which to Salvius?

As the last part of the story contains some complex sentences, it is suggested that students should go over it before embarking on the questions for discussion. They could work in pairs on lines 10-29, one student translating Salvius' speeches, the other Haterius' speeches and the stage direction at the end.

### Discussion

*Status.* Which would you prefer, **spēs immortālitātis** or **praesēns pecūnia**? Is Haterius being reasonable in wanting his name remembered long after his death? Did he achieve this ambition (cf. illustrations pp. 23 and 31)?

*Comedy.* How would you describe the character of the story **polyspaston** (pp. 29-30)? What elements in the story give you this impression, e.g. the depiction of Salvius, Haterius and even Glitus, the dialogue, the situation?

### Illustration

p. 31 Detail of two of the figures depicted on the mausoleum (p. 23). The snake (left-hand portrait), sometimes kept as a pet in the ancient world, often appeared on lararia to represent the benevolent spirit of the dead. It symbolises immortality because in shedding its skin it appears to be reincarnated. It is also associated with gods of healing and still forms part of medical symbolism

## About the language 2: pluperfect passive tense (p. 31)

**New language feature**. The pluperfect passive is introduced by comparison with the pluperfect active, which was introduced in Stage 16.

**Discussion**. Start by picking out on p. 29 those sentences describing the crane which contain the pluperfect passive, for translation and discussion with students:

> ibi stābat ingēns polyspaston quod ā fabrīs parātum erat (lines 9-10).
> in tignō polyspastī sēdēs fīxa erat (line 10).
> Haterius fabrīs imperāvit ut fūnēs, quī ad tignum adligātī erant, summīs
> vīribus traherent (lines 17-19).

Elicit by questions the following points: Haterius and Salvius went into the yard (in the past). The workmen had prepared the crane *before* Haterius and Salvius entered the yard, and so the sentences describe a crane which *had been prepared* ... a seat *had been fixed* ... ropes which *had been tied* to the beam.

Then study p. 31, paragraphs 1 and 2. Note that the second part of the tense is the imperfect of **esse** and compare it with the ending of the pluperfect active. Put up the perfect passive **portātus sum**, so that students can comment on the formation of the two tenses. In introducing paragraph 3, remind students that pluperfect verbs usually occur in conjunction with other past tenses (as in the story) where they are easier to recognise. These examples are isolated and short to enable them to focus on the new form and learn it.

**Consolidation**. Using familiar vocabulary, provide examples for practising the perfect and pluperfect passive, e.g.:

> arcus, in quō figūrae sculptae erant, ante lūcem perfectus est.
> quamquam arcus ab omnibus laudātus erat, nūllum praemium Hateriō datum est.
> Vitellia, quod īrā marītī affecta erat, cōnsilium cēpit.
> Salviō polyspaston dēmōnstrātum est.
> polyspaston ā fabrīs parātum erat.
> sēdēs in tignō fīxa erat; fūnēs ad tignum adligātī erant.
> Salvius et Haterius igitur fūnibus ad caelum sublātī sunt.
> Salvius, quod magnopere timōre affectus erat, Hateriō dōnum prōmīsit.
> ambō ad terram ā fabrīs dēmissī sunt.

These sentences could be set for a written homework and kept for future reference.

Go over these sentences, asking students to state whether the participle is singular or plural and the reason. If you have not done so before, this would be a good moment to discuss the gender of the participle.

Continue in the coming stories to draw attention to passive forms of the perfect and pluperfect, and elicit a range of translations. There are more examples on p. 127.

## Word patterns: adjectives and nouns (p. 32)

**New language feature**. Abstract nouns ending in **-tās**, formed from adjectives.

**Discussion**. Ask students to work through the examples in pairs and discuss their conclusions.

**Illustration**. African mosaic (*Bardo Museum, Tunis*).

# Practising the language (p. 33)

*Exercise 1*. Translate the sentences and state whether the verb is present or imperfect, active or passive.
*Exercise 2*. Complete the sentences with the correct form of the participle.
*Exercise 3*. Complete the sentences with the pluperfect subjunctive by generating the most suitable personal ending. (You may receive a range of less obvious answers which should nevertheless be credited as long as students translate them correctly, e.g. **(b) spectāvissēmus; (c) īnspexissent; (e) vīdissem.**)

# Cultural background material (pp. 34-7)

**Content**. This section describes Roman building techniques, and explains how the invention of concrete made construction quicker, cheaper and more versatile.

**Discussion**. The following questions could also serve as headings for notes.

What would have been the roles of the contractor, architect and sub-contractors in building the arch of Titus?

What different kinds of workmen were needed?

What tools were available to Roman workmen? How did they differ from modern tools? (Very little except that there were no power tools. See the illustrations on pp. 32 and 36.)

Why did you need a skilled crew to erect and work a crane?

Explain the difference between cement and concrete.

How did the Romans conceal the concrete core of their buildings?

## Illustrations

p. 34 •   A series of wooden 'profiles', made by a carpenter, with planks fixed across them, support the arch until the keystone makes it self-supporting. The architect designed the arch with a stone projection to support the wooden frame in order to avoid the use of scaffolding.

p. 36 •   Trowel (*St Alban's Museum*), left upside-down in a lump of concrete. The wooden handle has rotted away leaving the spike and metal collar (left).

p. 37 •   Winter baths, Thuburbo Maius, Tunisia (top left).

•   Dome of Pantheon (bottom left) has a hole 9m across, the only source of light inside the building, with a brickwork ring acting as keystone of the vault. The dome is built in horizontal layers of different materials, e.g. comparatively light volcanic rock towards the top. The coffers were originally enriched with stucco mouldings, painted and gilded, with a bronze flower at the centre of every panel.

•   The picture at bottom right illustrates a similar mixing of materials. The Colosseum (top right) was constructed by first building all the stone pillars (A) and the wall (B) round the outside, like a scaffold, then fitting the rest in between - a good system for working rapidly with relatively untrained workmen.

p.38 • Brick stamp (*British Museum*), AD 139, second consulship of Antoninus Pius with Balbinus as colleague (IMP ANTONINO II E(t) BALBIN COS). Bricks are helpful in dating buildings, though they were not always used immediately they were made and were sometimes re-used. The rest of the inscription:

D(E) P(RAEDIIS) Q(VINTI) S(ERVILII) P(VDENTIS) D(OLIARE) O(PVS) ARABI SER(VI)

This indicates that the slave (SER) potter Arabus (ARABI) made the brick on the estates of Quintus Servilius Pudens. The archaeologist cut out the stamp and threw away the rest of the brick.

## Checklist vocabulary: cognates and compounds

(diēs) nātālis, nōbilitās, remittere, timēre, timidus.

## Suggested activities

1 Imaginative writing: Imagine yourself to be Haterius' foreman, Glitus, and write a first-hand account of the building of the arch, including the final efforts to get it finished on time.
2 Consider the arch of Titus (pp. 15 or 24) or the tomb of the Haterii (pp. 23, 31 or 35). How many occupations or trades would be involved in producing the finished object? They could be represented in a diagram, showing the links between the people concerned, from Haterius to the quarryman cutting out the first block of stone. Supporting tradesmen, e.g. waggoners, bargemen, would also need to be represented. This could be done very effectively on computer.
3 Make a small diagram or model of Haterius' crane. (Lego may be available in the Design and Technology Department.)
4 Identify buildings where concrete would have been used in the construction.

# STAGE 31 in urbe

| Cultural background | Story line | Main language features | Focus of exercises |
|---|---|---|---|
| The city of Rome, its splendour and squalor.<br><br>Patronage: duties of patrons and clients; the **salūtātiō**. | Euphrosyne, a Greek female philosopher sent for by Haterius' life-style adviser, disembarks and walks through Rome to Haterius' house. Arriving at the time of the **salūtātiō**, she is rebuffed by the herald and her slave is assaulted. She counsels patience. | • Ablative absolute.<br><br>• **nē** in indirect commands and purpose clauses.<br><br>*Word patterns*<br>Compound verbs with **ā-, circum-,** and **in-**. | 1 Perfect and pluperfect passive.<br><br>2 Singular and plural forms of nouns.<br><br>3 Selection of correct verb, noun or participle. |

## Opening page (p. 39)

**Illustration**. Docker transporting amphora from merchant ship (right) to river boat (left) for transport to Rome (*detail from mosaic in Square of the Corporations, Ostia*). Note the mast (left) which was used for attaching towing ropes, and the fact that the docker is going across a plank laid between the ship and the boat. A more complete picture of a riverboat can be seen on p. 51.

## Model sentences (pp. 40-1)

**Story**. A typical day on the Roman waterfront. A ship berths, dockers unload its cargo of grain onto the quayside, the captain pays them off, and they make for the nearest pub. As night falls, they leave the pub the worse for wear, all money spent.

**New language feature**. Ablative absolute.

**New vocabulary. illūcēscēbat, saccāriī, expōnere, magister** (new meaning), **distribuit, occidere.**

**First reading**. First clarify what the line drawings are showing, so that students tackle the Latin with a correct idea of the story line, e.g.:
*Sentence 1*. What time of day is it?
*Sentence 2*. Where are we?
*Sentence 3*. What has arrived? What are the sailors on the right doing?
*Sentence 4*. What is happening in this picture?
*Sentence 5*. What is the captain doing?
*Sentence 6*. Where are the men going?
*Sentence 7*. What time of day is it now?
*Sentence 8*. What are the men doing here? What has happened to the contents of the bag in drawing 3?
    Read sentences 1 and 2 in Latin and ask for a translation, and repeat the process for each subsequent sentence. Understanding usually comes easily as each ablative

absolute follows a complete sentence describing the same occurrence, e.g. **diē illūcēscente** follows **diēs illūcēscēbat**.

Students often suggest a range of translations for the ablative absolute (*After the grain was unloaded ..., Once ..., Since ..., Because ...,* etc.), and all correct translations should be accepted.

**Discussion**. At second reading, put up one or two examples of the ablative absolute and, beside them, all the acceptable translations which are offered. Invite comments and encourage students to recognise that the phrases

1   are in the ablative case;
2   are a 'shorthand' in Latin, which needs to be extended in English with words
    that make sense of the sentence, e.g. *while, when, after, since,* etc.

Then ask students to translate the remaining examples. If necessary, use clues in the drawings to establish the correct relationship between the two parts of the sentence, e.g. 'When did the captain pay the dockers?' 'When did the dockers leave the pub?'

If students have difficulty in translating the present participle, e.g. in sentence 8, ask them if the sun has already set or is still doing so, and elicit the translation *was setting*. Recognition of the present participle and a literal translation of the phrase, *with the sun setting*, may also help.

**Illustrations**: Schematic drawings showing the Tiber dockside at Rome, with a warehouse behind and, in 5 and 6, a bar.

## adventus (p. 42)

**Story**. Arriving by ship from Greece, an attractive girl with a letter for Haterius makes her way through Rome in the early morning.

### First reading
*Paragraphs 1-3:*
Set the scene by discussing the illustration of the quayside scene (see note below) comparing it with the photographs on p. 51.

Ask for the meaning of the title **adventus** and then read the first paragraph aloud in Latin, pausing after each phrase to ask a question or to request a translation, so that students quickly gather a significant amount of meaning during the initial reading. At the end of the paragraph ask a question that makes students summarise or reflect on the paragraph as a whole, e.g. 'What would strike you about Rome so early in the day?'

Continue with paragraphs 2 and 3 in the same way. After paragraph 2 bring the new characters to life by asking students for their impressions of the drawing on p. 44. Speculate on the contents of the letter to Haterius. At the end of paragraph 3 ask: 'What was the girl's first reaction to the Subura? What was going on there to account for this? What impression do you have of the girl in lines 16-19?'.

Students could then make individual translations for discussion in the next lesson, choosing paragraphs 1-2, or paragraph 3.
*Paragraph 4.* Read in Latin with expression, and then ask students to work out a translation in pairs. Encourage them to guess the meaning of unfamiliar words before looking them up, and underline those they do look up. As you move round

helping the pairs, you will be able to make a note of common words they did not recall, for later vocabulary practice.

**Discussion**

1 Read **The city of Rome** (pp. 51-5) and trace Euphrosyne's route on the plan (p. 52). The questions on p. 44 of this Guide may be used as a basis for discussion and as headings for notes.

2 Return to **adventus** and ask students to find words used by the writer to convey:
  *the life of the poor*: **pauperēs ... traherent** (lines 13-14), **mendīcī ... postulantēs** (lines 14-15), **aliī ... dēnsa** (lines 21-3);
  *the noise of the city*: **clāmōribus hominum** (line 11), **mendīcī ... postulantēs** (lines 14-15), **fabrī clāmāre coepērunt** (lines 15-16), **verbīs scurrīlibus appellāvērunt** (lines 16-17);
  *the difficulty of movement*: **tanta ... prōcēderet** (lines 11-12), **dīvitēs ... lectīcīs vehēbantur** (line 14), **mendīcī ... circumveniēbant** (lines 14-15), **multī ... contendēbant** (line 20), **eīs ... dēnsa** (lines 22-3), **hūc illūc ... obstābant** (lines 25-6).

3 Compare this daytime scene with the picture of Rome at night (**nox I**, p. 4) making two lists of contrasting activities, perhaps subdivided into those of rich and poor.

4 Which aspects of the scene would you find in a great city today and which only in ancient Rome?

**Consolidation**

Ask for a translation of the imperfect passives (**expōnēbātur**, line 3; **dūcēbantur**, line 4; **portābantur**, line 8; **vehēbantur**, line 14) and the pluperfect passive (**importātī erant**, line 4) and use them as a basis for oral practice keeping the person and voice constant, but varying the tense, e.g. 'If **portābantur** means *they were being carried* what does **portātī sunt** mean?'.

Put up for translation and discussion examples of the ablative case with the verb: **multitūdine clāmōribusque ... obstupefacta est** (lines 10-11); **dīvitēs ... lectīcīs vehēbantur** (line 14); **puellam verbīs scurrīlibus appellāvērunt** (lines 16-17).

**Illustrations**

p. 42 • A sea-going boat unloading at Tiber Island (called by the Romans **īnsula inter duōs pontēs**), with the Pons Fabricius (dates from 62 BC) in the background. Note the temple of Aesculapius, god of healing (no trace survives, but it was probably on the site of the church of St Bartholomew at the downstream end); and the downstream end of the island carved in the 1st century BC in the shape of the prow of a ship. The carving and the temple commemorate a miraculous event. After a plague the Romans sent to Epidaurus for the statue of Aesculapius. As the ship with the statue approached the island, a huge serpent was seen to leave it and swim to the island. The serpent was taken to be an incarnation of the god himself and the island thus became the site of the temple and the carving.

p.43 • Plan taken from the model (p. 1). The city grew up at the point where the Tiber island at the bend of the river (far left) made crossing easiest. The seven hills, though not obvious from this viewpoint, influenced the disposition of the city, e.g.:

      **a**    the Palatine Hill (overlooking the Circus in one direction, the Forum in the other) contained the imperial palace and government buildings of architectural splendour;

      **b**    the Esquiline and the other airy hilltops (bottom and far right) were occupied by the homes of the rich;

      **c**    the poor were crowded into the notorious area of the Subura (top centre left) and the low, swampy ground between the hills.

See also the plan on p. 52.

## **salūtātiō I (pp. 44-5)

**Story**. Arriving at Haterius' house, the girl and her slave watch the herald handling the throng of morning callers.

**First reading**. To help students appreciate this story, study 'Patronage' (pp. 56-7) in conjunction with it. The story can, if necessary, be broken down into four parts:

*First impressions, lines 1-6*: questions 1-4;
*The herald, lines 6 - 11*: questions 5-8;
*The fortunate, lines 12-23*: questions 9-12;
*The unfortunate, lines 24-9*: questions 13-14.

Question 15 asks students to pick out instances of the patronage system at work. It could be extended to general revision of the background section.

Read the passage in Latin before asking students to attempt the questions.

Answers and mark scheme are as follows:

**Marks**

| | | |
|---|---|---|
| 1 | At the first hour/just after dawn. | 1 |
| 2 | Some were hoping for kindness/an act of kindness, others for a handout of food or money. | 2 |
| 3 | On the edge/at the back of the crowd. | 1 |
| 4 | (She was wondering) why so many men were standing there at that hour. | 2 |
| 5 | The herald was huge and fat; had an arrogant face and spiteful eyes. | 3 |
| 6 | The clients started to shout. | 1 |
| 7 | They begged the herald to let them in to their patron. | 1 |
| 8 | He may have been waiting until the shouting died down/he may have enjoyed keeping the clients in suspense/showing his power over them *or similar*. | 1 |
| 9 | The clients all have three names. | 1 |
| | A freedman would have included the name of his patron in his name. | 1 |

10 They were pleased they had been chosen from the crowd/they
   wanted to show (the herald and) Haterius that they were eager
   to carry out their duties, probably hoping that they would be
   rewarded in some way *or similar*.                                    1
11 They remained, keeping their eyes fixed on the herald.               2
   They were hoping for some favour *or similar*.                        1
12 The herald put **ad cēnam** first to capture the clients' attention,
   as they would all want to be invited to dinner/He left the
   names of the three clients right to the end, so that everyone
   was kept in suspense.
   *Accept any sensible answer*.                                         1
13 He enjoyed the sight of the clients fighting for the money/he
   wanted to humiliate them/there were not enough coins to give
   the clients one each *or similar*.                                    1
14 **immōta**; **attonita**.                                             2
15 **Two of**: Witnessing accounts; escorting the patron to the forum;
   possibly advising the patron about a building (C. Rabirius
   Maximus (line 23) is an architect).                                   2
   Inviting clients to dinner.                                          1

                                                              TOTAL $\overline{25}$

## Discussion

This is a good place to explain the use of **nē** in indirect commands and purpose
clauses. Put up the example in the story: **clientēs, nē sportulam āmitterent, dēnāriōs
rapere temptāvērunt** (lines 26-7) and ask students to translate and identify the
purpose clause. Follow this up with the previous example of an indirect command:
    hic … fabrīs … imperāvit nē labōre dēsisterent (**nox II**, p. 4, lines 5-7)
and, if there is time, with two further examples:
    dē morte patris … nārrāre nōlēbam nē vōs quoque perīrētis (p. 6, lines 16-17)
    servum iussit festīnāre nē domum Hateriī tardius pervenīrent (p. 42, lines 18-19)
Then turn to 'About the language 2' p. 50. See p. 44 of this Guide.

**Consolidation**. To draw attention to the ablative absolutes, ask students to find the
Latin for: with their eyes fixed on the door (line 2), with her slave standing at her
side (line 3), when the door suddenly opened (line 7), after seeing the herald (line 9),
when everyone was silent (line 12), after hearing their names (line 17), their eyes
fixed on the herald's face (line 18), after saying these words (line 26).
    Collect expressions of time: **prīmā hōrā** (line 1), **illā hōrā** (line 5), **nōnā hōrā** (line
22), **tertiā hōrā** (line 25) and remind the class of this use of the ablative. Ask them for
the approximate modern equivalents of the Roman hours (see p. 16 of this Guide.
Balsdon, *Life and Leisure in Ancient Rome*, pp. 16-18 gives an interesting detailed
account.
    Ask students to look at the sentences containing **sē** (lines 10 and 27), and **suās**
(line 13) and **suīs** (line 17), and work out who is being referred to in each case.

## salūtātiō II (p. 46)

**Story**. The herald shuts the door, refusing admission to any more visitors that day. The slave knocks and introduces his mistress as a philosopher summoned from Greece by Eryllus, Haterius' lifestyle adviser. The herald derides Eryllus and knocks the slave down.

**First reading**. Take the story in two parts, breaking at line 12. Read each section dramatically in Latin and ask students to tell you what they have gleaned from the reading. Then read it aloud again and ask them to explore the section in pairs. They may need help with lines 1-3, especially the dative **praecōnī regressō**; lines 14-16 and 24-5. You could put a mixture of hints on the board, e.g.:

> lines 1-3. Who returned? Who spoke to whom?
> lines 14-16. Eryllus epistulam ad Chrȳsogonum scrīpsit. Eryllus Chrȳsogonum
>     rogāvit ut philosopham mitteret.
> lines 24-5. nōlī dēspērāre!
>     dēbē**mus**
> necesse est nōbīs crās revenīre.

Divide the class into groups of four and ask them to give a dramatised reading in Latin or English. You need a narrator, slave, herald, and Euphrosyne.

### Discussion

1   Why did Euphrosyne come to Rome?
2   Why did the herald refuse to admit her?
3   What did the herald think of Eryllus? What was Eryllus' job? (Note: the Emperor Nero had an **arbiter ēlegantiae** whose job was to keep abreast of fashion and advise his master.) How do people learn about fashion and taste these days?
4   How often does the herald use the word 'order' or 'command'? How do you think the herald got away with this behaviour to Roman citizens? Where might Haterius himself be at this time of the **salūtātiō**?
5   What do you think of the various pieces of advice Euphrosyne gives to her slave after he was thrown in the mud?
    Note on Euphrosyne: She is a fictional character, based on a historical figure mentioned in the following inscription which was found in Rome (*Inscriptiones Latinae Selectae* 7783):

| | |
|---|---|
| EVPHROSYNE PIA | *Good Euphrosyne (Greek name means Joy)* |
| DOCTA NOVEM MVSIS | *learned in the nine muses* |
| PHILOSOPHA | *a philosopher* |
| V(IXIT) A(NNIS) XX. | *lived 20 years.* |

### Consolidation

Pick out the following sentences containing a dative and ask the class to translate them: **servō puella imperāvit** (line 2), **praecōnī regressō servus ... inquit** (lines 3-4).

Augment these, if necessary, with examples from **salūtātiō I**, e.g. **cēdite aliīs** (line 22), **cēdite architectō C. Rabīriō Maximō** (line 23), **cēterīs nūntiāvit praecō** (line 24). See the noun tables on pp. 114-15 for revision of the forms and p. 135 for the uses of the dative. Further examples of the dative with a participle, placed first in the sentence (like **praecōnī regressō**), are given on pp. 136-7, para. 5.

Find a few minutes for revision of the imperative based on **abī** (line 5) and **nōlī vexāre** (line 24); and of the gerundive with **redeundum vōbīs est** (line 11) and **nōbīs reveniendum est** (line 25). The use of the gerundive with transitive verbs will be introduced in the next Stage.

A translation of **admittitur** (line 5) and **missa est** (line 8) could lead to oral practice by substituting different endings and tenses, e.g. 'What would **admittēbātur** mean? And **admittēbantur**? Give two translations of **missī sunt**. How would you translate **admissī erātis**?' etc. This might be a good moment to consolidate the number and gender of the participle by studying paragraphs 8 and 9, p. 127.

**Illustration.** Note the ring on the door for attaching the guard dog.

## About the language 1: ablative absolute (pp. 47-8)

**New language feature.** This section focuses initially on examples of the ablative absolute containing perfect passive participles, before presenting examples with present and perfect active participles.

**Discussion.** Take the note at one sitting, for coherence and simplicity.

In tackling paragraph 3, encourage students to produce first a literal translation and then a variety of translations for each ablative absolute, e.g. (**3d**) *Their leader being killed …, When their leader was killed …, Since their leader was killed …, After the killing of their leader … .* Encourage flexibility between active and passive, e.g. (**3b**) *Having lost her money … .*

If students enquire about the term 'absolute', explain that the Latin means 'detached' or 'untied'. Demonstrate, perhaps with the sentences in paragraph 3, that each sentence makes sense without the ablative absolute, which is unconnected (i.e. not tied in) to the structure of the rest of the sentence. It does no harm to point out that the absolute phrase is not confined to Latin but occasionally occurs in English, e.g. **3f** which could be translated *The door shut, the clients,* etc.

## Word patterns: compound verbs 2 (pp. 48-9)

**New language feature.** Compound verbs formed with the prefixes **ab-**, **circum-** and **in-**.

**Discussion.** Ask students to work through the section on their own and go through it later. Draw attention to the variation in **ab-** ( **au-** or **ā-**) and elicit an explanation by getting students to say **abferre** and **auferre** to one another and to comment on the ease or otherwise of the pronunciation. Repeat with **inmittere/immittere** and **inrumpere/irrumpere**. Also refer to the common Latin device of stating the preposition and repeating it in the prefix of the verb, as in **3b**.

## Practising the language (p. 49)

*Exercise 1.* Complete the sentences by selecting the correct form of the perfect or pluperfect passive verb.
*Exercise 2.* Change highlighted nouns from singular to plural.
*Exercise 3.* Complete the sentences with the correct Latin word, selecting by sense and morphology.

## About the language 2: nē (p. 50)

**New language feature**. nē + subjunctive in indirect commands and purpose clauses.

**Discussion**. This note may be studied after **salūtātiō I** (see p. 41 of this Guide).

Take paragraphs 1 and 2 together, letting students work out a couple of the examples for themselves before you check them, then repeat the process with paragraph 3.

## Cultural background material (pp. 51-7)

**Content**. The section on the city of Rome is best taken with **adventus**, p. 42, and that on the daily duties of patrons and clients with **salūtātiō I**, pp. 44-5).

**Discussion questions**

*The city of Rome*
1  Why did Rome grow up where it is?
2  Why did the rich people choose to live on the hills? What were their houses like? Where did they go in the summer?
3  What made living between the hills less pleasant for the rest? Why did they have to live in unsafe flats rather than live further away from the centre of the city? Where did they spend their leisure hours?
4  Where did Romans get their water for drinking and washing? Where did the waste end up? What made the water and sewerage systems possible?
5  Why was it difficult to sleep in Rome?
6  If you lived in Rome, where would you go:
   a  for a cheap haircut (Subura);
   b  for a summer evening stroll away from the crowds (Campus Martius);
   c  to pray for a cure from illness (temple of Aesculapius on Tiber Island);
   d  to watch a chariot race (Circus Maximus);
   e  to hear an open-air political speech (Rostra in the Forum).

*The system of patronage*
1  What were the duties of clients?
2  What were the responsibilities of patrons towards their clients?
3  On the evidence of the stories in Stages 29-31, who would you prefer to have as your patron, Haterius or Salvius? Give your reasons.
4  What, if any, were the advantages of the Roman system? For instance:
   a  poor citizens had some financial support, e.g. sportula;
   b  poor citizens had someone to speak up for them in court;
   c  ex-slaves, e.g. Clemens, gained a start in independent life;
   d  the needs of small communities were met, e.g. Pliny at Comum;
   e  patrons gained the service and status which they needed.
5  What were the disadvantages? For instance:
   a  you needed influence, rather than ability, to make your way;
   b  clients could be exploited and abused by threats to withdraw help, or compulsion to do something unacceptable (compare the power of the mafia);
   c  the system bred hypocrisy and dishonesty, e.g. poets and their patrons.
6  Does patronage exist today? For instance, sponsorship.

**7** What is today's system for supporting poor people? Is it better or worse than the Roman system?

## Illustrations

p. 50 • Top: wharf, 2nd century AD, on the bank of the Tiber. Originally three tiers of barrel-vaulted warehouses ran along the riverside.

• Below: Monte Testaccio, Rome. This hill, 20,000 sq m at base, was constructed behind some warehouses entirely from Spanish and North African oil amphorae, which were imported in vast quantities. It was not just a tip but was carefully arranged and maintained, with raised terraces, retaining walls, and cart tracks up the sides. The amphorae were carried up whole by donkeys, smashed on the spot (see handle at centre left of photograph) to accommodate the largest possible number, and sprinkled with powdered lime to neutralise the stench of rancid oil. The deliberate smashing suggests that oil amphorae could not be re-used like wine amphorae.

p. 51 • View of the Tiber island looking upstream. At the centre, in front of buildings, is the carving representing a ship sailing out to sea. The hospital on the island continues the tradition of healing (see p. 39 of this Guide). The bridges are: (back left) Pons Cestius; (right) Pons Fabricius; (foreground) Pons Aemilius (Ponte Rotto) as rebuilt by Augustus. This originally had six arches, of which one survives, together with a fragment of its neighbour.

• Painting from Ostia (*Vatican Museums*). A river boat with two steering oars at left, mast towards front (the usual position for boats which were towed by animals), and saccarii coming up the gangplank. With the help of the caption get students to identify the name of the boat (far left), her master, Farnaces (on cabin top), and Arascantus who is supervising a slave pouring corn into a **modius** (fixed measure for corn) from a sack which is labelled **rēs** (goods, stuff). The dark figure on his right holding a branch (or tally stick) is checking the cargo of corn.

p. 52 • Relief of shop scene (*Ostia Museum*). Poultry hang from a beam. In cages below are live chickens, rabbits or hares. On the counter above are monkeys (to keep the children amused), vegetables in flat baskets, and a tall basket with holes, possibly for snails (one, barely visible, is escaping, top left of basket). A customer at left is holding a duck or chicken.

• Blacksmith's shop, relief on a smith's gravestone (*Museum at Aquileia*). The figure at left is blowing the bellows through a screen to protect him from the heat of the forge (centre), while the smith (right) works with tongs and hammer at the anvil. The hearth is raised on a platform of stone or brick, the fire is covered by a hood, raised into a pediment, to control the draught. Elicit these points from students, giving them clues, if necessary.

p. 53 • Trajan's markets, part of the development round Trajan's forum, possibly started by Domitian. These shops, with doors framed in travertine (a light-yellow porous rock) for status, are much grander than anything in the Subura, with its tortuous, narrow roads, and timber buildings which were unhealthy and unsafe. The photograph (top right) gives the effect of a multi-storey Rome (the upper three floors on the right are later, though the rest is original).

p. 54 • Colosseum looking along the wider axis of the oval towards the gladiators' entrance, with emperor's box just off left (north), public marble seating rising in tiers, and underground works below main arena, including animal cages, man-turned pulleys for raising them, ramps for scenery, etc. The Roman building was further complicated by later uses; see *The Ancient City* by Peter Connolly and Hazel Dodge.

• Circus Maximus, with people (right) giving sense of scale. In the centre is the **spīna** at the ends of which were the **mētae** (turning posts). On top of the spina were egg-shaped or dolphin-shaped lap counters: the eggs were removed, and the bronze dolphins dived at the end of each lap. See bottom drawing, p. 78, top picture, p. 91, and the notes on pp. 60 and 68 of this Guide.

p. 55 • Aqua Claudia, with (on top) Anio Novus, crossing the Campagna near Rome. Started by Caligula, it was finished in 52 AD by Claudius. The river Anio runs from its source in the hills and debouches into the Tiber north of Rome, but these aqueducts drew the water in a purer state from a point far upstream. A settling tank was installed to cut out the mud, which still recurred when it rained.

p. 56 • Marcus Holconius Rufus in military dress, marble statue from Pompeii (*Naples, Archaeological Museum*). Five times duovir, he served in the army, and had a career in Rome. In Pompeii he paid for improvements to the temple of Apollo and the Great Theatre.

p. 58 • Drain cover, or fountain head, in the porch of S Maria in Cosmedin, Rome. It depicts the head of a river god, recognisable by the horns, symbolic of the river's power. The location is on the line of the Cloaca Maxima, in the Forum Boarium.

## Checklist vocabulary: cognates and compounds

altitūdō, dēspērāre, dūcere, ēvolvere, ōrātor, spēs, superbē.

## Suggested activities

1   *Puzzle*: A soldier earned 300 denarii (1200 sesterces) a year. How many days would you have to attend your patron's salutatio to earn as much? Would you be better off as a soldier, or as Haterius' client? This activity could follow the reading of **salūtātiō I**, pp. 44-5.
    Note: A client who attended the salutatio and collected the sportula on 192 days out of the 365 could get as much as the soldier earned over the 365 days. But the sportula could not be depended on. A client might turn up at the salutatio day after day and receive no sportula at all, if his patron (or his patron's slaves, as in the story on p. 45) were so inclined.

2   Using the pictures in this Stage as your starting-point, compile a Visitor's Guide to Domitian's Rome, with paragraphs on: Arriving by sea; Where to find a good night's sleep; The baths, water and sanitation; In a medical emergency; Leisure activities; The riverside; Shopping; The heart of the city. A useful book is *A Visitor's Guide to Rome* by L. Sims. (The teacher could help students to compile

a list of useful Latin phrases for tourists, including some on the topics above, but also on asking directions, eating out, making friends, etc.)

3   Prepare for Test 1. Revision will not only help you with the Test, but will reinforce what you have learned so far.

    **a**  From each Stage you have read choose one story to re-read carefully, asking for help with any sentences or phrases you find difficult;

    **b**  Read through the model sentences, and the sections headed 'About the language'; select some of the examples to translate and ask for help with any difficulties;

    **c**  Look over any work you have done on the cultural background information, noting carefully the comments and advice from your teacher.

# STAGE 32 Euphrosynē

| Cultural background | Story line | Main language features | Focus of exercises |
|---|---|---|---|
| The structure of Roman society.<br><br>Some Roman popular beliefs: astrology, Stoicism and Mithraism. | Finally admitted to entertain the guests at Haterius' birthday party, Euphrosyne tries to explain Stoicism with the story of a poor man who was content in adversity because of his virtue. Finding the story incomprehensible and boring, the guests end up fighting over Euphrosyne. | • Deponent verbs.<br><br>• Gerundives of obligation: transitive verbs.<br><br>• Future ticiples.<br><br><br>**Word patterns**<br>4th declension nouns and related verbs. | 1 Agreement of adjectives.<br><br>2 Changing direct to indirect commands. |

## Opening page (p. 59)

**Illustration**. Portrait of a woman from Hawara, Roman Egypt, mid-2nd century (*Manchester Museum*). Encaustic on panel. She has pearl earrings and a necklace of green stones. Whether Euphrosyne would have worn jewellery is questionable; virtually all Roman women did.

## Model sentences (pp. 60-1)

**Story**. Denied admission to Haterius' house and refusing to bribe the herald, Euphrosyne decides to return to Greece. The same day, Haterius' birthday, Eryllus comes to report to his master.

**New language feature**. Deponent verbs, here restricted to the perfect tense. Students have met perfect active participles since Stage 22, but will encounter the term 'deponent' for the first time in 'About the language 1'.

**First reading**. Get the class to recall the events in **salūtātiō II**, p. 46, perhaps by reminding them of some of the phrases, including the reference to Eryllus. Then give a Latin reading of each model sentence in turn, and invite translation. All the deponents have already been met in participial form and so, with glossing and line drawings, translation is straightforward.

**Discussion**. Why did Euphrosyne fail to gain admission to Haterius' house? What do you think will happen as a result of Eryllus' arrival?

Postpone discussion of the new feature until 'About the language' on p. 64, unless students volunteer comments or ask questions. Concentrate on correct translation.

**Consolidation**. For homework, ask students to write a translation of some or all of the model sentences. Subsequently, oral practice of phrases incorporating the deponent verbs provides useful consolidation.

## ** Euphrosynē revocāta I (p. 62)

**Story**. Eryllus tells Haterius about the plans for his birthday dinner; the entertainment, in the form of an attractive, female philosopher, will make him a leader of fashion. When Haterius asks where the girl is, Eryllus suspects that the herald may have refused her admission.

**First reading**. Introduce this passage with a lively Latin reading, followed by questions to draw out the meaning and significance, e.g.:

How did Eryllus address Haterius (lines 1-2)?

**omnia … parāta sunt** (line 3) **… nihil neglēctum est** (lines 6-7). What do these two sentences mean? Make a list of the actions that have been carried out by Eryllus. What does Haterius notice has been missed out?

**hominēs … optimus quisque** (lines 10-12). Which words in this passage do you think Eryllus emphasises? Find an appropriate English rendering of **eiusmodī**, **urbānīs** and **nunc**. Read the speech in Latin and English with suitable facial expression. Was the speech effective in persuading Haterius?

**at domine … missa est** (lines 15-18). What has Eryllus obtained? What three 'selling points' does he list for Haterius?

**optimē fēcistī, Erylle** (lines 19-20). Why was Haterius so pleased with Eryllus? What question does Haterius ask (line 21)?

**anxius** (line 22). Why is Eryllus right to feel anxious? What does he fear has happened?

Does this story agree with your prediction of what would happen?

### Discussion
1  What kind of celebration did Haterius plan for his birthday? What do you think he hoped to gain?
2  Why does Eryllus plan to introduce a philosopher? What is Haterius' general view of philosophers?
3  Discuss the contrast in character and style between the smooth, efficient and sophisticated slave and his wealthy but uncultivated master.

**Consolidation**. Ask students to re-read the story in pairs and prepare a Latin reading.

## Euphrosynē revocāta II (pp. 62-3)

**Story**. The herald admits what he has done and is sent to fetch Euphrosyne who is already boarding the ship for Athens. With difficulty he persuades her to return with him.

**First reading**. Read the first three lines in Latin and ask volunteers to translate. Elicit literal and idiomatic translations of **poenās maximās eī minātus est** (line 2).

Divide the class into groups of three, to share out the parts of the herald, Haterius and Euphrosyne within the group. Ask them to listen with care to your Latin reading of the rest of the story, and then to work out the meaning of the passage for themselves, tackling the narrative passages together. Go over the story by asking for volunteers to translate the various parts and narrative. Invite the rest of the class to comment on the translations and to correct them, if necessary.

**Discussion.** Why did the herald go to such lengths to persuade Euphrosyne to return? Had he been wrong in thinking that his master had no interest in philosophy (p. 46, lines 10-11)? Why did Euphrosyne give in to him? Was this an appropriate decision for a philosopher?

**Consolidation.** Ask students to find the ablative absolutes, reminding them that they are looking for participial phrases in the ablative case, which can be omitted without changing the sense of the sentence: **tōtā rē nārrātā** (line 3), **nōmine audītō** (line 12), **effūsīs lacrimīs** (line 19). These three examples, each with different endings, provide an opportunity, if needed, to revisit the different ablative endings tabulated on pp. 114-15.

This is a good place to consolidate the pronoun **is**. Pick out the following examples:

> (Haterius) poenās maximās eī minātus est (line 2).
> (praecō) ... magnā vōce eam appellāvit (lines 11-12).
> (Euphrosynē), precibus lacrimīsque eius commōta, domum Hateriī regressa est (p. 63, lines 20-1)

Ask students for a translation of the sentences and the cases of the pronoun; enter them on a grid on the board or the OHP and see if students can supply further forms before turning to the table on p. 122.

Note the explanation of the adjectival use of **is** (p. 122) and discuss the literal meaning of **hominēs eiusmodī** (**Euphrosyne revocāta I**, p. 62, line 10).

Compare the forms of **is** with those if **īdem** (p. 122) and do the exercise in paragraph 5. Elicit the rule that **īdem = is + dem** and ask students to spot and account for the exceptions: 'Say **eumdem** and **eundem** to your neighbour and explain the form **eundem**'.

As preparation for 'About the language 1' (pp. 64-5), pick out the deponent verbs, and ask students to translate them: **praecō ingressus est** (line 1), **minātus est** (line 2), **philosopha ... profecta est** (line 6), **regressa est** (line 21). Note whether students deal confidently with the examples where there is no expressed nominative.

## cēna Hateriī (pp. 63-4)

**Story.** Haterius' many guests, including a consul, are delighted with the lavish and ingenious food, and the vintage wine. To a fanfare of trumpets Euphrosyne is led in, introduced, and asked to perform.

**First reading.** It is helpful to read the section on Roman society (pp. 71-2) in preparation for this story. Take the story at a good pace, using Latin reading and easy comprehension questions to cover the ground quickly, and to help with the meaning of the imperfect and pluperfect deponent verbs, which appear here for the first time. The following questions may then be used to ensure that students understand the meaning of a sentence as a whole and the force of various details. The story can be divided into three parts:

*The guests, lines 1-9*

> What time of day was the ninth hour? What were Haterius' friends and clients doing at this time (lines 1-2)?

Which two Latin phrases in line 3 describe the change that had occurred in the lives of the freedmen's sons? What effect does the writer achieve by putting the phrases next to each other?

Why were senators among Haterius' guests (lines 4-5)?

Who was reclining next to Haterius (lines 6-7)? What kind of man was he?

In what ways was Haterius trying to impress him (lines 7-9)? Do you think he was likely to succeed?

*The banquet, lines 10-19*

While this was going on, what were the two Ethiopians doing (lines 10-11)?

Who had followed them? What was his job? (lines 11-13)

**aprō perītē sectō ... pīpiantēs** (lines 13-14). What details in this sentence are illustrated in the drawing above? Why is the sound of the word **pīpiantēs** particularly appropriate?

What was the effect of the cook's prowess on the guests? on Haterius? What was Haterius' next act? (lines 14-17)

What announcement did the steward make (lines 18-19)? What is the significance of the word **Hateriānum**? What do you think of the description on the label **vīnum centum annōrum**? What do these phrases tell us about Haterius?

*The entry of Euphrosyne, lines 20-32*

**digitīs concrepuit** (line 21). Why did Haterius do this?

How did Haterius make Euphrosyne's entrance impressive (lines 21-3)? Can you think of any modern equivalents?

What was the effect of her appearance on the guests (line 24)?

Pick out the two present participles in lines 25-7, and translate them. What do they tell us about Haterius' attitude to Euphrosyne?

Which word in Haterius' final speech (lines 31-2) do you consider the most hypocritical?

## Discussion

1   How would you describe Haterius' dinner-party? Is it funny, pathetic, vulgar, incredible? Quote examples from the passage to support your view. (Some details of the dinner are taken from Petronius, *Cena Trimalchionis*).

2   Look at the chart of Roman society (p. 71). Where would you place Haterius? From which sections of society do his guests come? (**clientēs**, line 1, suggests that some might have been plebeians.)

**Consolidation.** Set students to write a translation of lines 1-13 (**nōnā ... secāret**).

Ask students to pick out the subjunctives and explain why they are used: **celebrārent** (line 2), **secāret** (line 13), **vīdissent** (line 14), **parāvisset** (line 15), **īnferrent** (line 17), **cōnsīderet** (line 26). This activity could be supported by further work from pp. 138-9.

Practise translating ablative absolutes: **aprō sectō** (line 13), **amphorīs inlātīs** (line 17), **hospitibus ... bibentibus** (line 20), **signō datō** (line 21).

This story contains several examples of the genitive case. Ask for translations of: **fīliī lībertōrum** (line 3), **favōrem Hateriī** (line 5), **vir summae auctōritātis** (lines 6-7), **spē favōris** (line 7), **amphorās vīnī Falernī** (line 16), **vīnum centum annōrum** (lines

18-19), **aliquid philosophiae** (lines 31-2). Revise the forms and uses of the genitive on pp. 114-15 and 135 respectively, if necessary.

It is worth spending a few minutes on revising **ferō**, using **ferēbant** (line 11), **īnferrent** and **inlātīs** (line 17) as the way into discussion. The verb is best explained as an amalgam of different verbs, like 'go/gone', 'wend/went' in English. The verb forms are set out on pp. 132-4; students have already met some of the compounds on p. 48.

## About the language 1: deponent verbs (pp. 64-5)

**New language feature.** Present, imperfect, perfect and pluperfect tenses of deponent verbs. Note: the present tense is introduced for the first time in this language note. Before embarking on the note make sure that students can translate examples of the perfect tense of deponent verbs in context, drawing them from the model sentences, **cēna Hateriī** (lines 24 and 26) or **Euphrosynē revocāta**.

### Discussion

1   Study the examples in paragraph 1. Students should now readily recognise **locūtus est** and may be able to account for its form and that of the imperfect, which has occurred less frequently, before reading the explanation. Note the term 'deponent' and examine the imperfect and perfect in the table in paragraph 2, eliciting comments on the formation of the tenses. Then ask students to pick out the examples of the imperfect deponents in **cēna Hateriī**, retranslating the complete sentences: **ingrediēbantur** (line 2), **adloquēbātur** (line 8), **ingrediēbantur** (line 10).

2   Subsequently set students to retranslate this sentence from **cēna Hateriī: statim coquus, quī Aethiopas secūtus erat, ad lancem prōgressus est ut aprum secāret** (lines 11-13). Elicit comments on the tenses of **secūtus erat** and **prōgressus est** e.g. by asking 'Which happened first?'. Study the examples of the pluperfect in the table on p. 64, comparing it with the perfect tense.

3   Examine the forms of the present tense. The examples in paragraph 3 could then be set as written work.

  Only the third person forms of deponent verbs are given in the table. The perfect and pluperfect tenses are set out in full on p. 130, but leave consideration of these until later.

4   Reassure students by stressing that there are only a few deponent verbs in Latin, that they have met most of the common ones already and that the context of the sentence is usually helpful. (They will be given a list later on p. 110.)

**Illustration.** Detail from another part of the model of ancient Rome (p. 1), showing part of one of the hills on the outskirts of Rome which was occupied by wealthy people with houses set in gardens and parks.

## philosophia (pp. 66-7)

**Story.** Euphrosyne tells a story of a poor man who is patient in adversity because he is a Stoic. It fails to convince the diners. The consul tries to kiss her and a fight ensues. She leaves, deploring the gluttony and lust of the rulers of the world.

**First reading**. Take the story in sections, varying the method so that pace and momentum are sustained, e.g.:

*Only the mad work, lines 1-7.* Read this in Latin with expression, merely asking the class to tell you what picture they have of the poor man, what Apollonius said, and what kind of man he was.

*A dig at Haterius? lines 8-12.* After your reading, ask the class to translate this section in pairs and go over it.

*Moderation versus extravagance, lines 12- 21.* Invite volunteers to tell you in English what Euphrosyne said about the poor man in lines 13-14. Use leading questions to ensure the class has understood the sense of the rest of this section, especially the force of the gerundives in lines 16-17, e.g. 'How did Balbus describe the poor man? What ought not to happen?'

*Stoicism in adversity, lines 21-31.* After your reading, ask students to make a list of all the misfortunes that beset the poor man (lines 22-5). What kind of death did he have? What is Euphrosyne's comment? Is it surprising?

*An excitement greater than philosophy, lines 32-43.* A dramatic reading should be enough to convey the meaning of this passage. If necessary draw up a list of the actions which occur in lines 39-43.

*Parthian shot, lines 44-8.* A lively reading should suffice, but ask the class to unpick Euphrosyne's final words.

**Discussion**. Questions might include:

1   Why are the guests **obstupefactī** by what Euphrosyne says in lines 9-10? Do you think her words were deliberately aimed at Haterius?

2   **ille pauper ... fēlīx erat** (lines 28-9). Which two words contrast sharply with each other? Where else does Euphrosyne use a paradox (line 46)?

3   What did Euphrosyne as a Stoic believe the aim of life should be? What did her Stoic beliefs lead her to believe was the best sort of society? Is Euphrosyne's view of life rather naïve, as her simple story might suggest? What impression of her do you gain from her final comment (line 46)?

4   For what qualities does Euphrosyne praise the poor man in her story? Do you agree with her?

5   What does Haterius try to do during the fight? With what success? What had been his intentions in holding the party? Do you think he has achieved them?

Ask the class to read the section on Roman beliefs (pp. 73-5), then divide them into small discussion groups of three or four and allocate one of the questions on p. 67 to each group. Draw together their conclusions in a full class discussion. Students should be encouraged to supply reasons and evidence for their views.

1   The following points may be made:

   a   Haterius' guests were not interested in philosophy. They had come to enjoy an extravagant meal and have a good time.

   b   The guests could not understand how a poor man who had lost his family, farm and freedom, could still be content.

   c   Euphrosyne was naïve; she had no knowledge of the guests and did not realise they would not be interested in the life of a poor man which was so different from their own.

**d** Her way of telling the story did not stimulate her audience except as a basis for some crude remarks.

**2** The point that Euphrosyne was trying to make was that the poor man was content because he did not rely on the material world or other human beings, but had a clear conscience and the knowledge that he had done his best all his life. Euphrosyne is choosing a very extreme case to make the point that inner contentment does not depend on external circumstances. Although one may object to the example, her remark is not a stupid one.

**3** Euphrosyne attended a dinner whose guests included a consul and wealthy men, examples of Romans who were the masters of the world. However they had no control over themselves as they were slaves to gluttony, drunkenness and lust. This is shown by their behaviour at the lavish banquet provided by Haterius and their treatment of Euphrosyne as a sexual object.

**Consolidation**
Set half the class to write a translation of the story which Euphrosyne told (lines 2-5, 13-14, 22-9); and half to translate the scene of the riot: **sed priusquam … cōnābātur** (lines 32-43). As you go over the written work with the whole class, ask students to give the meanings of the deponent verbs: **adlocūta est** (line 1), **cōnābātur** (line 14), **passus est** (line 22), **patiēbātur** (line 26), **mortuus est** (lines 27-8), **passus est** (line 31), **cōnābātur** (line 43), **adlocūta est** (line 45), **profecta est** (line 48). Ask them to identify who performed the action, and, in the case of the perfect tenses, how this affects the form of the verb.

Put up examples of phrases containing 4th declension nouns: **plausū audītō** (lines 19-20), **multōs cāsūs** (line 22), **tot cāsūs** (line 31), **vultū serēnō** (line 44). Get students to work out the case and number. (This activity could lead on immediately to further work on 4th declemsion nouns in 'Word patterns', p. 68.) Repeat this process with 5th declension nouns: **spē favōris** (line 9), **rē vērā** (lines 10 and 28-9), **rēs adversās** (line 26).

Select from the following list any pronouns in need of revision and discuss them in context: **sibi** (line 4), **eī** (line 9), **ille, nōbīs** (line 16), **huic** (line 19), **haec** (lines 21, 36 and 39), **ipse** (line 24), **ille** (line 28), **eum** (line 30), **eī** (line 32), **eam** (line 38).

# About the language 2: more about gerundives (p. 67)

**New language feature**. The gerundive, which has previously occurred in the impersonal form, is now introduced in agreement with nouns. Focus on the sentence pattern, rather than on the gerundive alone.

**Discussion**. The transition from paragraph 1 to paragraph 2 is quite small, and students have met several examples of the new feature in **philosophia** (pp. 66-7). Ask students to complete the examples in paragraph 3 on their own so that you can check their understanding. The gerundive forms of the four conjugations are given on p. 129. Discuss the use of English in 'referendum', 'agenda', 'Amanda', etc.

**Consolidation**. Find all the sentences containing a gerundive in **philosophia** and translate them.

## Word patterns: verbs and nouns (p. 68)

**New language feature.** Fourth declension nouns associated with verbs. Let students tackle paragraphs 1-3 on their own.

**Consolidation.** Put up some phrases for translation, e.g. **metū mortis, cursus honōrum, rīsū ēbriō, mōtū nāvis, spē cōnsēnsūs, lūctum magnum**. Supply a context for the more difficult phrases and refer students to the table on p. 114, if necessary.

## Practising the language (pp. 68-9)

*Exercise 1.* Complete the sentence by working out the correct form of a given adjective.

Elicit the point that adjectives agree with their nouns in case, number and gender, but do not necessarily have the same ending. Extend this exercise by revising adjectives, pp. 116-17, and doing the exercises on p. 117.

*Exercise 2.* Pairs of sentences: (1) Translate a direct command; (2) Complete the indirect command generated from it with the correct form of the imperfect subjunctive, referring to p. 128 if necessary.

## About the language 3: future participles (p. 70)

**New language feature.** Future participles.

**Discussion.** Read paragraph 1 with students and then let them attempt the examples in pairs or individually. Encourage a wide range of translations, e.g. *I am about to give you …, going to give you …, intending to give you …,* etc.

In studying paragraph 3 elicit the information that the future participle is formed like the past participle with **-ūr-** inserted, and that it is active in meaning. The derivation of English 'future' from **futūrus** may help some students.

**Consolidation.** Collect examples from previous reading for students to translate:

nōs omnēs crās moritūrī sumus (p. 6, lines 18-19).

Imperātor Domitiānus eō diē arcum dēdicātūrus erat (p. 9, lines 3-4).

Haterius praemium ā Salviō acceptūrus erat (p. 9, line 11).

Euphrosynēn in nāvem cōnscēnsūram cōnspexit (p. 62, **Euphrosynē revocāta II**, line 11).

These could be modified to give further practice if necessary.

## Cultural background material (pp. 71-5)

**Content.** The section on Roman society is best taken with **cēna Hateriī** (pp. 63-4), and that on astrology, philosophy and other beliefs with **philosophia** (pp. 66-7).

**Discussion**

*Roman society*

Students could be divided into three groups, each taking one of the classes in Roman society and preparing answers to questions 1, 2 or 3 below. When they have reported back, all students could discuss questions 4 and 5. They could write up a neat version of the answers to questions 1-5 as a permanent record.

1   How did most senators achieve their rank? What kind of work was open to them? What kind of work do you think they looked down on (e.g. earning a

living openly, especially by trade)? What privileges did senators have? What made Agricola and Salvius exceptional members of the senatorial class?

2 How did men become equites? What kind of work was open to them? What privileges did they have? Why might some equites refuse promotion to the senatorial class (e.g. desire to avoid the risks and toils of a political career at the higher level; preference for being a distinguished eques rather than an undistinguised senator; wish to continue in commercial life from which senators were barred by law and convention)?

3 What opportunities were there for ordinary Romans to make a living? What help was there for the poor?

4 From the stories of Haterius' household what picture do you have of the way Roman society worked? What attracted senators to Haterius? What did he gain from them?

5 Look at the information below. Do you think the gap between rich and poor was greater then than it is today? Was there any way of levelling it out in ancient Rome? What is the effect of modern tax systems on wealth and poverty?

| Qualifications of classes | Some of the evidence we have |
|---|---|
| **Senators** <br> *Qualification*: property of one million sesterces, giving annual income of approx. 50,000 sesterces, if we assume 5% interest. | Pliny called himself 'not rich' with property of 20 million. <br> Regulus, his rival: 60 million. <br> Seneca, the emperor's tutor, exceptional at 300 million. <br> Narcissus, the emperor's freedman, exceptional at 400 million. |
| **Equites** <br> *Qualification*: property of 400,000 sesterces, giving annual income of approx. 20,000 sesterces. | Income from 400,000 sesterces regarded as 'modest but comfortable' by Juvenal. |
| **Plebs** <br> *No property qualification*: estimated average income of labourer: 800 sesterces for 200 working days per year. | A centurion earned per year approx. 6,000 sesterces, a legionary 1,200. (For a comparison between a legionary and a client receiving the sportula, see p. 46 of this Guide.) |

*Roman beliefs*
1 What systems of belief might Romans follow beside the state religion?
2 What do you know of their attitude to astrologers (recall Stages 19 and 20)?
3 Why did Mithraism become popular in the army?
4 What other religions came to Rome from the East (recall Stage 19 for Isis)?
5 The Romans turned to new religions and philosophies to answer questions about life, e.g. What are justice, truth, love? What is a good society? Can people answer these questions any better today?

**6** What do you think were the principles which guided Haterius and Salvius in the way they lived their lives? Are there people like them today?

**7** Do we have people like Euphrosyne today talking about serious questions for a public audience?

**Illustrations**

p. 71 • Curia Julia as built by Julius Caesar, and subsequently restored in AD 283 after a fire. This building survived in its entirety because it became a church. The outside would have been covered with marble on the ground floor and stucco above. Note the holes in the brickwork where the roof beams of the colonnade were attached along the front of the building.

p. 72 • Mosaic from hall of **mēnsōrēs** (guild of corn-measurers) at Ostia (see the picture on p. 51 and also p. 45 of this Guide). It shows a mensor with a modius in front of him, and a stick in his hand with which to level off the grain in the modius. A slave (left) carries a full sack on his shoulder, while another slave stands next to the mensor counting the number of sacks or measures by stringing tags onto a stick.

p. 73 • Planisphere (a two-dimensional representation of the heavens), with the figures representing the seasons, from the Villa Marco, Stabiae (*Antiquarium, Stabiae*).

p. 74 • Head of Chrysippus (*British Museum*).

p. 75 • Temple of Mithras which was in an apartment block (insula), and is now under the church of S. Clemente, Rome.

p. 76 • Relief of Mithras slaying the bull (*Museum of London*). To the left and right stand minor deities, Cautes and Cautopates: one with torch raised, the other with torch pointing down. The symbolism of the scene is disputed, but it may have represented the struggle between the forces of good and evil, light and darkness, death and rebirth in nature. There seems to have been a strong connection with astrology, hence the signs of the zodiac in the border. Students may enjoy identifying them.

## Checklist vocabulary: cognates and compounds

dēpōnere, īnfundere, lībertus, paupertās, revenīre.

## Suggested activities

**1** *Group discussion* (could lead to imaginative writing):

**a** Work out a story for Euphrosyne to tell Haterius and his guests which would have a better chance of convincing them that *Virtue is better than Pleasure or Riches.*

**b** Work out what impressions of Rome Euphrosyne would report to Chrysogonus on her return to Athens. What would have impressed her, and what would she criticise?

**c** Look at the two meanings of **aequus** (p. 76), and make a list of all the associated English words you can find which are derived from the Latin word.

2 *Evidence*: Read these translations of poems by the Roman poet Martial, and answer the questions below:

a   Five whole days I wanted, Afer, on your return from Libya,
    To pay you a friendly visit, just to say Hello.
    'He's busy', I'm told, or 'He's sleeping', as I come a second, a third time.
    Enough of that, then, Afer. You don't want Hello, so - Goodbye.

                                                                        (IX, 6)

b   I accidentally called you Caecilianus one morning,
    Your real name, not 'My lord'.
    You ask what such liberty costs me?
    That lost me a whole hundred - peanuts!                             (VI, 88)

c   For three denarii, Bassus, you send me an invitation
    First thing to put on my toga, and then to gaze at your atrium,
    And then to stick to your side, to parade in front of your litter,
    To visit wealthy widows, ten of them, more or less.
    My toga's threadbare, Bassus, it's skimpy and it's old.
    For three denarii, Bassus, I can't buy a toga.                     (IX, 100)

What point is Martial making in each of these poems?
What is the mood of each poem?
What do you think he expected to be the result of his poems?
What do you think the effect of the poems on his patrons would be?

# STAGE 33 pantomīmus

| Cultural background | Story line | Main language features | Focus of exercises |
|---|---|---|---|
| Christianity.<br><br>Entertainment: theatre, chariot-racing, gladiatorial fights, private entertainment. | A Christian preacher interrupts a performance by Paris, the pantomime artist, in Haterius' garden. When Paris performs for the empress, the emperor's freedman tries to arrest him for misconduct with her, but the attempt is foiled. | • Future active.<br><br>• Future perfect active.<br><br>*Word patterns*<br>Diminutives. | 1 Ablative absolute.<br><br>2 Conversion of sentences from active to passive form. |

## Opening page (p. 77)

**Illustration.** Wall painting from Herculaneum (*Naples Archaeological Museum*). An actor in his dressing room, wearing the costume of a king in tragedy: long white robe with sleeves, golden band round his chest, purple mantle over his knees. He holds a sceptre and his dishevelled hair suggests that he has just taken off his mask which is now resting in a shrine (right). Paris could well have looked like this, but the mask of a pantomimus did not have an open mouth as he spoke no words. Note that the pantomimus was a serious performer in an elevated form of drama comparable to classical ballet.

## Model sentences (pp. 78-9)

**Story.** Three heralds announce the entertainments that will take place the following day in the theatre, the circus and the amphitheatre.

**New language feature.** Future active.

**First reading.** Give a dramatic reading of the three announcements or get three good readers to do so. Ask them to emphasise **crās** in each set of sentences, This is usually sufficient for students to identify that the events described are to happen in the future. If not, use comprehension questions to lead students to a translation, e.g.:
    Who are the three men shown in the illustrations?
    What are they announcing?
    When will these shows take place?
Translate their speeches.

**New vocabulary. pantomīmus, tībiīs, cantāre** (new meaning), **duodecim, aurīgae.**

**Discussion.** Rely on **crās** to guide students to a correct translation of the verb, accepting any appropriate English version, e.g. '*... will perform a play*', '*... is going to perform a play*', etc. If students comment, confirm that the verbs are future. Otherwise postpone discussion until 'About the language' (p. 85) .

**Consolidation.** Divide the class into three and set each group to write out a translation of one of the groups of sentences; then go through the sentences orally.

**Illustrations**. Discuss the line drawings in detail, eliciting as much factual information about the three forms of public entertainment as possible, e.g.:
1  *Theatre*. An impressionistic representation showing raised stage, typical architectural **scaenae frōns**, semi-circular orchestra where senators sat, and the ceiling over the stage area only, to act as a sounding board. The figures represent Paris and Myropnous, who appear in the stories of this Stage. Pantomime had a musical accompaniment provided by singers who sang the words of the story.
2  *Circus Maximus*, seen from the emperor's box which was opposite the finishing line. The emperor has a palm branch which he will award as a prize to the winner. Note the spina with the three metae (turning posts) and the lap counters in the shape of eggs. Three laps have been completed, four remain, and slaves stand by with ladders to remove the eggs. One of the four chariots has crashed. Reins can be seen tied behind the waist of the nearest charioteer.
3  *Flavian amphitheatre (Colosseum)*. Gladiatorial fight between retiarii and **secūtōrēs**. The latter, like the murmillones in Stage 8, were often matched against retiarii. A dead body is being hauled off (left).
Follow up these discussions by studying the model of central Rome (p. 1) which shows the position of the Colosseum and Circus Maximus and two theatres: Pompey's theatre at top left, and the theatre of Marcellus on the left, near the Tiber. Then read 'Entertainment' (pp. 89-91). The section on the theatre gives the context for the stories in this Stage.

## Tychicus (pp. 79-80)

**Story**. In Haterius' garden Vitellia's friends idolise Paris and rhapsodise over his performance, but are interrupted by a Christian, Tychicus. He chides them for worshipping anyone but the one true God and proclaims the doctrines of Christianity as he is thrown out.

**First reading**. The story can be broken down into sections for students to explore individually or in small groups, e. g.:
*Paris mimes the death of Dido, lines 1-8*: Read the section aloud in Latin, and explain the story of Dido. Then ask students to write a translation in small groups. Compare and discuss their translations.
*The interruption, lines 9-15*. Read in Latin and ask comprehension questions, e.g.:
> While Paris stood up to acknowledge the applause, what happened (lines 9-10)?
> What did the man look like (lines 9-10)?
> What did the audience do (lines 11-12)?
> **paucī eum agnōvērunt** (line 12)? What did they know about him?
> What effect did the interruption have on Paris (lines 13-14)?
> Why was he at a loss (lines 14-15)?
*The declaration, lines 16-22*. Put the following questions on the board or duplicate them in advance so that they act as clues to students about what to look for.
> What did Tychicus criticise the audience for doing (lines 16-17)?
> What reason did he give (lines 17-18)?
> What did the spectators do (line 20)?
> What question did some of them ask (lines 20-1)?
> Why did others summon the slaves (lines 21-2)?

*The statement of belief, lines 23-28.* Read Tychicus' speech expressively once or twice. It may be familiar to some students from the Christian Creed; if so, ask them for the wording in the Creed.

*The prophecy, lines 29-39.* After the Latin reading, ask the group to describe what was happening to Tychicus while he made this speech. Help them to start translating the prophecy (which has echoes of *1 Thessalonians* 4. 16-17), laying emphasis on **mox** to highlight the future, and then set them to complete it in pairs, before going over it.

*The reaction, lines 40-3.* Work through the last paragraph with the class, encouraging them to comment on the way Tychicus was treated and the varied responses of different groups of people.

## Discussion

1 *The death of Dido.* Dido, Queen of Carthage, killed herself as her lover Aeneas sailed away to fulfil his destiny of founding Rome. This scene (*Aeneid* Book IV, 642-92) was famous in the Roman world.

Translations are available by David West in Penguin Classics (prose) and by C.H. Sisson in an Everyman edition (verse). It is impossible to convey adequately the resonances, the pathos of the poetry, the tragedy of love lost, and, for a Roman, the cost of the founding of Rome. Perhaps most effective, for anyone with access to a CD player, is to play the beginning of Dido's famous lament, 'When I am laid in earth', from Purcell's opera, *Dido and Aeneas* (written to be performed by London schoolgirls in 1689).

2 *Historical authenticity.* Tychicus is fictional but his patron, Titus Flavius Clemens (see Stage 38) is historical. He was a cousin of Domitian who was put to death for 'atheism', which probably refers to Judaism, possibly Christianity.

3 *Christianity.* After reading the story and studying p. 81, use questions to help students to understand the events and background of the story, e.g.:

  a What Christian beliefs and practices are described? (Early Christians proclaimed the peace and love of Christ, but also predicted in an urgent and prophetic style the imminent end of the world, and the judgement which would follow.)

  b How were Christian beliefs about life after death different from Roman ones (recall details of Book I, Stage 7)?

  c Why were Christians unpopular at this time? (Reasons include:
    they refused to worship the Roman gods as well as their own, or combine their god with Roman god, thus inviting the wrath of the gods on the whole community;
    their meetings were regarded as suspicious by the authorities, fearing political subversion. Even companies of firemen were banned under Trajan;
    since Christians and Jews frequently clashed at this time, they were seen as a threat to civil peace;
    phrases from Christian services were misinterpreted, e.g. 'This is my body, take, eat ...' 'Love one another').

  d Why were Christians often confused with Jews? What is the difference?

  e Whose message do you think would be the more comforting to the poor and wretched, Euphrosyne's (p. 66, lines 2-29) or Tychicus'?

**f** If students ask about the official acceptance of Christianity, key events and emperors are: Edict of Toleration 311, Constantine (324-37), the first Roman emperor to worship Christ along with the Roman state gods, Theodosius (379-95), the emperor who made Christianity the state religion.

**Consolidation.** Set students to re-read the story for homework, listing any queries for explanation in the next lesson.

Ask them to explain the force of **ipse** (line 13) and **ipsī** (line 43).

Different groups could be asked to find, translate in context and explain to the rest of the class examples of:

**a** *The forms and uses of subjunctives*, e.g. **ut ... exciperet** (line 8), **ut stāret** (line 14), **quis esset et quid vellet** (lines 11-12), **quid factūrus esset** (line 15), **utrum ... faceret an īnsānīret** (lines 20-1), **quī ... ēicerent** (lines 21-22), **cum prōnūntiāvisset** (line 40).

Note that **priusquam ... ageret** (line 9), is the first example of **priusquam** with the subjunctive. Save discussion and consolidation until more examples have been met.

**b** *Phrases with the ablative case*, e.g. **admīrātiōne** (line 6), **statūrā brevī vultūque sevērō** (lines 9-10), **magnā vōce** (line 10), **nōmine** (line 13), and ablative absolutes: **oculīs ... conversīs** (line 11), **fābulā interruptā** (line 13), **signō datō** (line 29), **magnō ... comitante** (lines 33-4). For further practice use exercise 1, p. 87.

**c** *Participial phrases*. In addition to the ablative absolutes in **b** above, this story affords good practice with participles in other cases, e.g. **morientis** (line 5), **affectī** (line 6), **prōgressus** (line 10), **suffīxus** (line 26) **clāmantem** (line 31), **missae** (line 38). Further practice is provided on pp. 136-7.

**d** *Perfect passives and deponents*: **factus est** (lines 23-4), **pollicitus est** (line 25), **mortuus est, positus est** (line 26), **vīsus est** (line 27). This is a good opportunity to remind students that context usually distinguishes passives from deponents.

**Illustrations**

p. 80 • The Chi-Rho symbol was often used in early Christian art. It consists of the two letters (Ch and R) which begin the Greek word, Christos (the anointed), which became associated with Jesus at an early stage.

p. 81 • Detail from a 4th century statue of a seated Christ teaching (*Museo Nazionale Romano, Rome*). No description of Christ is given in the Gospels; the sculptor borrowed conventions associated with gods of other mystery religions prevalent at the time.

• Centrepiece of large mosaic pavement, Hinton St Mary, Dorset, made by Dorchester craftsmen (*British Museum*). It shows Christ's head with the Chi-Rho symbol and two pomegranates, symbols of immortality. Curiously, it is the only known portrait of Christ on a pavement to be walked on, though it is common to put pagan gods on pavements. The same pavement also depicts a pagan story (which however may have been interpreted in a Christian way as a story of good and evil).

## in aulā Domitiānī I (pp. 82-3)

**Story.** As Paris performs for the empress, she is warned that Epaphroditus is arriving with soldiers. Paris escapes onto the roof, his pipe player hides behind a tapestry, and Domitia pretends to be listening to a recitation by her slave.

**First reading.** Take a few moments to look at the line drawing of the atrium in Domitian's palace. Can students identify the room? What are its distinguishing features?

The story and questions may be tackled in the following way:

*Lines 1-13 with questions 1-7.* Take orally with the class and give help, if necessary, with three sentences: **in scaenā ... agēbat** (lines 1-2), **nūllī ... habēbat** (lines 4-6) and **subitō ... ingressus est** (lines 9-10).

*Lines 14-29 with questions 8 and 9.* Explain that you will read these lines aloud twice. Between your readings students should study questions 8 and 9, which will help their understanding by focussing attention on particular sentences. Remind them that the form of the question and the marks allotted give clues to what is expected in their answers. Give them time to study the lines and write down their answers.

*Lines 30-35 with questions 10 and 11.* Follow the same procedure suggested for lines 14-29.

*Question 12.* This could be discussed orally in class and followed up by a dramatised reading of the dialogue (lines 15-29) to bring Paris' personality to life. Answers and mark scheme are as follows:

|  | | Marks |
|---|---|---|
| 1 | In the/an atrium of Domitian's palace. | 1 |
| 2 | The story of the love of Mars and Venus. | 1 |
| 3 | Myropnous. He was a dwarf and a friend of Paris. He was playing sweetly. *Give a half mark for 'Myropnous' and for each of three other points.* | 2 |
| 4 | One. | 1 |
| 5 | a   **oculīs in eō fīxīs.** | 1 |
|  | b   **(ut) lacrimās retinēre (Domitia) vix posset.** | 1 |
| 6 | Olympus had been ordered to guard the door of the atrium. | 1 |
| 7 | He had (just) seen Epaphroditus (the freedman of the emperor) crossing the courtyard, accompanied by ten soldiers. He would soon enter. | 3 |
| 8 | If Epaphroditus found Paris with her, he would certainly be punished. He would order his soldiers to throw Paris into prison. | 3 |
| 9 | Domitia's rooms were often searched; her letters were read; her slave-girls were questioned every day. | 3 |
| 10 | Paris hid on the roof, Myropnous behind a tapestry. | 2 |
| 11 | (Domitia remained) on her couch. | 1 |
|  | She had composed her features and ordered Olympus to recite some lines. | 2 |

**12** Possible answers include: Paris is
*Brave* in not being frightened by Epaphroditus.
*Lighthearted/has a sense of humour*: he smiles when he
hears Epaphroditus is coming/he says Domitia is
lucky because Epaphroditus wants to visit her.
*Contemptuous* of Epaphroditus, calling him Domitian's
parrot and a feeble little man (**homunculus**).
*Confident/adventurous*, shinning up a column to hide
on the roof. He seems to enjoy the risks he is
taking in having (or seeming to have) an affair
with the emperor's wife.
*Accept any character trait supported by evidence from the story.*     3

TOTAL $\overline{25}$

### Discussion
1   Why would the story of the love of Mars and Venus (p. 89) be an exciting drama
for Paris to perform to the empress? Of what would his performance consist?
What was the role of Myropnous?
2   Why was the freedman Epaphroditus so powerful? How did he show his power
in the treatment of the emperor's wife? Who would help him carry out the
activities described in lines 24-6?
Note: Paris was the stage name of the most celebrated pantomimus of his day, who
seems to have come from Egypt and was a favourite in the imperial household. His
affair with the empress is mentioned in Suetonius' *Life of Domitian*.

Domitia, daughter of Nero's most successful general, Cnaeus Domitius Corbulo,
married Domitian in AD 79 and was given the title Augusta when he became
emperor in AD 81.

Epaphroditus was a freedman who became the secretary in charge of petitions,
first of Nero and later of Domitian. He was one of a group of powerful imperial
freedmen who were in charge of important departments of state.

Myropnous is based upon a tombstone relief of the late 2nd century AD (see
p. 101).

**Consolidation.** If the long final sentence (lines 33-5) has caused problems, it may
need unpacking with comprehension questions (cf. p. 140) or the form of analysis
suggested on p. 16 of this Guide.

The passive verbs (lines 24-6) offer an opportunity for practice. The class could
be asked the meaning of **inspiciēbantur, īnspecta sunt**, etc. This is a good time to
undertake exercise 2 (p. 87).

**Illustration.** Line drawing of Paris escaping from an opulent imperial atrium with
impluvium and compluvium.

## ** in aulā Domitiānī II (p. 84)

**Story.** Epaphroditus sends for ladders to search the roof. Myropnous distracts him
and stuns him with the curtain pole. As the soldiers carry him out unconscious,
Myropnous puts a coin in his mouth and Paris declaims a mock epitaph.

**First reading.** Take the story as a whole and maintain the pace so that the excitement and the humour come across. After a Latin reading, help students with comprehension questions, e.g.:

What was happening when Epaphroditus entered?

What question did he put to the empress (lines 3-4)? Is there anything that surprises you in the way he spoke to her?

How did Domitia reply (lines 5-6)? With which word did she give herself away?

How did Epaphroditus encourage the soldiers to redouble their efforts (line 11)?

Why did Domitia go pale at Epaphroditus' words in line 12?

What plan did Myropnous initiate in lines 14-15?

What was the tone of Epaphroditus' words in lines 17-18? What did he expect to happen next?

Which two words (line 20) indicate that Myropnous kept his cool? What did he do and what happened to Epaphroditus (lines 21-3)? How did Myropnous show his feelings (lines 23-4)?

Where were the soldiers while this was happening? What did Domitia tell them to do (lines 26-7)?

What did Myropnous put into Epaphroditus' mouth (line 28)? Why? (A coin was the fare for Charon, the ferryman, who conveyed the souls of the dead across the river Styx to the Underworld; see Book III, p. 35.)

What is the meaning of **hīc iacet** (line 30)? What is the tone of this speech? Which words give it this tone?

Who has won in this encounter? What do you think will happen now?

### Discussion

1   What characters has Paris portrayed in this Stage? What personalities and situations were involved? What emotions did he evoke in his audience? Are there similar performers today?

2   Which point in the story do you think is the moment of greatest suspense? How is this achieved?

**Consolidation.** Ask students to produce individual translations of lines 19-31. Pick out the following examples of relative clauses from the story: **quem impudēns tū amās** (lines 3-4), **quī per tapēte prōspiciēbat** (lines 13-14), **quae sē iam ex pavōre recēperat** (line 25). Ask students to find the antecedent and explain the number and gender of the relative.

Students could also be asked to comment on the examples of the connnecting relative: **quae cum audīvisset Domitia palluit** (line 13), **quibus dictīs, Epaphrodītus ... sē praecipitāvit** (lines 19-20).

Follow up this exercise now or later by studying p. 123, which draws together the uses of the relative pronoun. After introducing paragraph 3, let students tackle the examples in pairs or individually before you go over them.

## About the language 1: future tense (p. 85)

**New language feature.** The future tense in the four conjugations and **sum**.

**Discussion.** Start by picking out a few familiar examples for translation (see the consolidation section below), putting the verbs up on the board, with their English translation. A particularly useful sentence to start with, since it puts present and future in close proximity, is **deinde … rēgnābit** (p. 80, lines 27-8). By now students will probably tell you that the new verbs are in the future tense, and should have no problems identifying the personal endings.

Read paragraph 1 and then look at the structure of the future tense in paragraphs 2 and 3. Compare the examples on the board with the forms in the tables. Note the unwelcome fact that the 1st and 2nd conjugations have different future forms from the 3rd and 4th conjugations, but do not at this stage complicate the issue by bringing up the similarities between the present tense of **doceō** and the future of **trahō**. Then get students to work independently on examples **a-e** in paragraph 4 and go over them. Be prepared to accept any appropriate English translation. For homework set students to learn to recognise the future forms of the four conjugations.

In a subsequent lesson, start with **f-g** in paragraph 4 as oral revision. Then study the future tense of **sum** in paragraph 5. This might be a good time to contrast it with the present and imperfect tenses of **sum** (see p. 132) and do a substitution exercise of the type suggested on p. 30 of this Guide.

**Consolidation.** Set students to pick out and translate examples of the future tense in stories they have read, e.g.:

> p. 80   **rēgnābit** (line 28), **iūdicābit** (line 34), **erimus** (line 36), **poenās dabis, erit** (line 37), **dēvorābunt** (line 39).
>
> p. 82   **intrābit** (line 13), **poenās … dabis, iubēbit** (line 19), **nōn capiet** (line 28), **abībō** (29).
>
> p. 84   **poenās dabitis** (line 11), **illum capiam** (line 18).

# Word patterns: diminutives (p. 86)

**New language feature.** Diminutive nouns.

**Discussion.** Let students tackle this section independently or in pairs, checking their answers with another student or pair, and simply bringing you any queries.

**Consolidation.** Check that students' queries have been clarified, and take any future opportunity to help them recognise the diminutive and its different uses:

- a factual description, e.g. **agellus** *a little field*. English examples might include, in addition to those in paragraph 5, statuette, rivulet, novella, gosling; students will no doubt supply more;
- a scornful comment, e.g. **mē nōn capiet iste homunculus** (Paris about Epaphroditus, p. 82, lines 28-9), **quid dīcēbās, homuncule?** (Modestus to Bulbus, Book III, p. 28, line 2); like English, 'You horrible little man' or 'the little woman'.
- an endearment, e.g. **ō libelle meus** (Martial sending his book of poems into the public domain), like English *baby, d(e)arling, Jimmy,* etc.

The examples in paragraph 2 show how English derivatives may have meanings which have travelled some way from the Latin original.

# Practising the language (p. 87)

*Exercise 1.* Complete the sentence by selecting the correct participle for the ablative absolute. Encourage variety in translation. This is a good exercise to use in consolidating **Tychicus** (pp. 79-80).

*Exercise 2.* In each pair of sentences, translate the first sentence and complete the second with the correct passive form of the verb to convey the same idea. The examples are in the present and imperfect tenses, and provide useful further practice after **in aulā Domitiānī I** (p. 82).

This is a good point to revise the passive forms, basing exercises on the types given on pp. 126-7.

## About the language 2: future perfect tense (p. 88)

**New language feature**. Future perfect tense.

**Discussion**. Study paragraphs 1 and 2 with the class, and then work through the examples in paragraph 4, referring to the table in paragraph 3 as necessary.

In discussion of the examples given, help students to observe that the future perfect tense always occurs here in combination with a future tense. It may be helpful to get the class to study the table on p. 125 to establish how the new tense relates to the perfect and pluperfect. Ask the class to make up a rule, which works in all four conjugations, for forming the future perfect. They wil be cheered to learn that they have now met all the six tenses.

**Consolidation**. It is less important to manipulate the conjugation than to give students practice in recognising and translating examples of the future perfect tense in the context of a sentence. Guide the class towards examples already met in the stories, ask them to identify the future perfect and translate the sentence in which it occurs, e.g.:

    p. 80    vīxerimus, crēdiderimus (line 35), dēstiteris (line 37).
    p. 82    invēnerit (line 19).
    p. 84    effūgerit (line 11).

In subsequent lessons, create short sentences for translation, using the future perfect and the future with **sī**, e.g.:

    sī ad urbem advēnerō, amīcum meum vīsitābō.
    sī mihi pecūniam reddideris, dōnum fīliō meō emam.
    mīlitēs, sī aulam dīligenter īnspexerint, Paridem invenient.
    sī lībertum adiūveris, tūtus eris.

## Cultural background material (pp. 89-91)

**Content**. This section is best studied with the model sentences. It reviews the three main forms of public entertainment in Rome: the theatre (introduced in Book I, Stage 5); chariot racing; the amphitheatre (described in detail in Book I, Stage 8). The last paragraph sets the context for the stories in the Stage by describing forms of private entertainment available to the wealthy.

**Discussion**. Ask students to read the text and study the pictures for themselves. Then lead into discussion by asking them questions about the pictures and exploring them further with the help of the notes on the illustrations below, e.g.:

What can you learn about chariot-racing from the pictures on pp. 88 and 91?

The pantomime actor in the top picture on p. 89 is holding three masks and has three different props. What characters do you think he is going to play? Why are the mouths of the masks closed? (See also the note on the opening page, p.59 of this Guide.)

How do you know that the seated figure in the picture on p. 77 represents a king?

How do you know that the figure at the top of p. 90 is a 'Thracian'? How many kinds of gladiators can you recall from Stage 8, and what were their characteristics?

Why do you suppose the senate chose to mint coins like the one on p. 92? How much of the Colosseum survives today? (See pp. 37 and 54.)

What entertainments do you think Domitia and Salvius might offer at their dinner-parties?

## Illustrations

p. 88 • opus sectile panel from a mid-4th century wall decoration in the basilica of Junius Bassus, Rome *(Museo Nazionale Romano, Rome)*, showing possibly the emperor, wearing the triumphal toga of purple and gold, leading the procession at the start of the chariot games in a two-horse chariot. The four factions are visible, sporting their colours (left to right): reds, blues, greens and whites. Domitian was obsessive about chariot-racing and later established two factions of his own, purple and gold. The riders here are possibly waving palm branches.

p. 89 • 4th century ivory from Trier, showing pantomimus with the masks and props of three characters: crown representing king; sword representing warrior; lyre, perhaps representing Orpheus *(Berlin)*.

• as on p. 77 (explained on p. 59 of this Guide).

p. 90 • Relief from a memorial in Chieti, showing the distinctive helmet of a 'Thracian' gladiator.

• Statue of acrobat *(British Museum)*, African by his hair and features, undertaking a daring trick in which some Egyptian acrobats specialised.

p. 91 • Terracotta relief, 1st cent AD *(Kunsthistoriches Museum, Vienna)*, showing a scene near the meta (turning point consisting of three obelisks) in the Circus. The chariot may have taken the turn too fast. It is the last lap, as can be seen by the fact that all seven dolphins have been turned into the diving position. The statue on top of a column, and the pavilion with battlements, are ornamental features on the spina (see photograph, p. 54). These small decorated plaques may have been sold as souvenirs.

• Terracotta relief , 1st century AD *(British Museum)*, showing a charioteer, reins tied round his waist, driving a four-horse chariot and approaching the meta. The obelisks were about 5 m high so that charioteers could see the meta above the clutter on the spina, and guage their distance from the turn. Having rounded the meta is a single charioteer on horseback, probably a **hortātor** (rather like a coach cheering on his protegé) rather than a competitor. The inscription on both plaques reads ANNIAE ARESCUSA and may indicate that they come from the workshop of Annia, and the place of origin.

p. 92 • A brass sestertius minted by the Senate to celebrate the opening of the Colosseum. Note how the arches are filled: the top storey has shields, the next two have statues, and the ground floor has entrances. Over the central (emperor's) entrance is a four-horse chariot. To the left is the Meta Sudans (sweating turning post), an ornamental fountain famous as a landmark, which survived into the 20th century when Mussolini demolished it to make way for his Processional Way. The object on the right has not been identified.

## Checklist vocabulary: cognates and compounds

dēicere, lūdere, numerāre, potēns, rēgnum, sī, vēritās.

## Suggested activities

1 Create the radio commentary for a visit to the races.
2 Read a translation of Ovid's day at the races, *Amores III.2.* from *Ovid in Love*, trans. Guy Lee or Ovid, *The Love Poems* trans. A.D. Melville.
3 Find out some of the symbols which were used as cryptograms and passwords by the early Christians when they were forced by persecution to go underground, e.g. the Chi-Rho sign (pp. 80-1); the cross, shameful as a gallows in the Roman world, but commandeered by Christians as a symbol for Christ; the fish, used because the Greek word for fish, ICHTHUS, is made up of the initial letters of the phrase 'Jesus Christ, Son of God, Saviour'; the word-square:

```
                              P
ROTAS                         A
OPERA               A    T    Ω
TENET                         E
AREPO                         R
SATOR               PATERNOSTER
                              O
                              S
                    A    T    Ω
                              E
                              R
```

For further information about the word-square, see *The Oxford Guide to Word Games* by A.J. Augarde, pp. 35-7.

**4** Find out what you can about the experience of Christians in the Roman world. An accessible piece of evidence is the narrative of the experience of Paul, a Jew with Roman citizenship, in the Acts of the Apostles: the Roman governor refuses to get involved in a Jewish-Christian dispute (chapter 18); the local souvenir sellers in Ephesus protest vigorously against his preaching (chapter 19); Paul claims the privileges of Roman citizenship, to the surprise of the Roman officer who has gained hs own citizenship through bribery (chapter 22); Paul appeals as a Roman citizen to Caesar (chapter 25).

# STAGE 34 lībertus

| Cultural background | Story line | Main language features | Focus of exercises |
|---|---|---|---|
| Freedmen. | Epaphroditus bribes Salvius to exact revenge on Domitia and Paris. By a trick, they are caught together in Haterius' empty house by the Praetorian Guard. In trying to escape, Paris falls to his death. Domitia is arrested lamenting over his body. | • Present passive infinitive. <br> • Future passive. <br><br> *Word patterns* <br> Compound verbs with **ad-, con-, prō-, trāns-** and **per-**. | 1 Future active. <br><br> 2 Selection of correct Latin words to translate an English sentence. <br><br> 3 Perfect and pluperfect passive. |

## Opening page (p. 93)

**Illustration.** Start by asking students to study this page and tell you who they think will play an important role in this Stage. Having established that it is Epaphroditus and that he is also the **lībertus** of the title, ask what they remember about him from the previous Stage (see also p. 74).

Can they identify the kneeling figure wearing the conical cap? some may remember from a relief in Book I, Stage 6 (p. 69), that he represents a newly freed slave, expressing his gratitude and sense of obligation to his ex-master. (The relief is reproduced in this Stage, p. 106.)

This illustration makes the point that freedmen like Epaphroditus might gain positions of considerable power but they owed them to their ex-masters, to whom they still had obligations. See the discussion section below.

Before embarking on the first story read the brief biography of Epaphroditus on p. 95 and explain the meaning of the inscription (see note on p. 72 of this Guide).

## ultiō Epaphrodītī (p. 94)

**Story.** With the approval of the emperor, Epaphroditus seeks revenge on Paris and Domitia. Finding it impossible to act openly, he bribes Salvius to set a trap for them.

**New language feature.** The future passive, 3rd person singular and plural.

**First reading.** Read lines 1-7 in Latin and elicit the meaning with comprehension questions, e.g.:
> What did Epaphroditus want to do, and why (lines 1-2)?
> What did the emperor urge Epaphroditus to do, and why (lines 2-4)?
> What was so difficult about this order for Epaphroditus (lines 4-6) ?
> What did he do about it (lines 6-7)?

Read the rest of the passage dramatically and ask students to translate it in pairs, raising any queries with you. Such is the momentum of the story, and the familiarity of the 3rd person passive endings, that students usually translate the new future passive verbs without difficulty.

## Discussion

1   *Epaphroditus.* Why was he so powerful? Note: The power he wields as a freedman may seem surprising, but several imperial freedmen gained positions of influence at court because of their closeness to the emperor. Linked to the emperor by gratitude and loyalty, they personally depended on him and were often regarded as more reliable and trustworthy than powerful senators who might be in control of an army and be potential rivals. Their power increased under Claudius and his successors when they were given important official positions, dealing for example, with petitions (like Epaphroditus) or judicial enquiries.

2   *Salvius.* Is Salvius' relationship with Epaphroditus better evidence of his closeness to the emperor than his statements on p. 30, where he tells Haterius he had consulted the emperor about his reward, and in Book III p. 97, where he declares he is better placed than Agricola to know the emperor's wishes about Cogidubnus?

3   When Salvius says **ēmovēbitur**, what does he really mean? This would be a good opportunity to discuss English euphemisms, e.g. 'taken out', 'taken care of'.

## Consolidation

Ask students in pairs to read dramatically the conversation between Epaphroditus and Salvius (lines 8-19).

Set them to find all examples of **ego** and **tū** and tabulate them on the board. Can they complete the tables? Do they remember the plurals? What do **mēcum, tēcum,** etc. mean? Refer to p. 120, if necessary.

Draw attention to the active infinitives, **difficile erat ... accūsāre** (lines 4-6); **pūnīre cupit** (line 9), in preparation for the introduction of the present passive infinitive in the next story. Revise the infinitive forms of the four conjugations.

**Illustration.** Part of an honorary inscription to Epaphroditus (*Museo Nazionale Romano, Rome*), referring to the fact that Epaphroditus had honours granted him for his part in exposing the conspiracy of Piso under Nero. It reads:

(A)VG · L · EPAPHRODIT(O · APPARITORI · CAE)SARVM · VIATORI · TRIBVNIC(IO · ...........HASTIS · P)VRIS · CORONIS · AVREIS · DONA(TO)
*To Augustus' freedman Epaphroditus, attendant of the Caesars, assistant to the tribunes. ... presented with pure spears and golden crowns.*

Epaphroditus was a common slave name and there were several imperial freedmen of that name. This inscription, however, was found in the area of the gardens owned by 'our' Epaphroditus, on the Esquiline, and therefore is more likely to refer to him than to someone else (*Inscriptiones Latinae Selectae 9505*).

Note that **Augustī lībertus** can refer to a freedman of any emperor. **hastae pūrae** were headless spears, which, like **corōnae aureae**, were given for valour in war. No doubt these honours were bitterly resented by Epaphroditus' enemies.

# īnsidiae I (pp. 96-7)

**Story**. Receiving a letter from Vitellia to say that she is ill, Domitia sets out on a foul night to visit her friend. The unoccupied house, brilliantly lit, with a banquet spread, leaves Domitia puzzled and her slave girl alarmed.

**First reading**. This is a useful passage for practice in independent work, and you could take students' answers in for marking. Explain that you will read lines 1-11 through in Latin at least twice. Between your readings they should study questions 1-6, which in themselves help understanding by focussing attention on particular sentences. Remind them that the form of the questions, and the marks allotted, give clues to what is expected in their answers. Questions 7-15 are more testing. With bright students repeat the same method as you used for the first half of the story, but with a slower class discussion in class should precede the request for written answers. Answers and mark scheme are as follows:

| | | Marks |
|---|---|---|
| 1 | She had (just) received a letter from Vitellia, the wife of Haterius. | 2 |
| 2 | Vitellia had become seriously ill *or similar*. | 1 |
| 3 | She must visit Vitellia. | 1 |
| 4 | Chione ordered a litter to be made ready and slaves to be summoned. | 2 |
| | She also sought a doctor to prepare medicines for Vitellia. | 2 |
| 5 | To Haterius' house. | 1 |
| 6 | It was a dark night and it was raining heavily. | 2 |
| 7 | The door was open. | 1 |
| 8 | The slaves were left outside the door. | 1 |
| 9 | Lamps were shining everywhere; garlands of roses were hanging from all the columns. | 2 |
| 10 | They were (completely) deserted. | 1 |
| 11 | The tables were heaped with very special dishes; the wine cups were full of very good wine. | 2 |
| 12 | She said they must beware; something strange was going on (there) *or direct speech*. | 2 |
| 13 | Domitia said that perhaps Vitellia had been taken ill while she was dining. | 2 |
| | Doubtless she was lying in her bedroom. | 1 |
| **14** | **ignāra īnsidiārum**. | 1 |
| 15 | Domitia may go to Vitellia's bedroom and find her dead/find the room empty/Salvius may have planned to get Paris to the empty house, so that he and Domitia may be caught together. *Any credible answer is acceptable.* | 1 |

TOTAL $\overline{25}$

## Discussion

1  *Domitia's behaviour*. How would you describe Domitia's response to her friend's letter? What did she find at the house that might have put her on her guard? How would you describe her behaviour: was she brave, or did she feel invulnerable as empress, or was she relying on the slaves outside the door, or was she too concerned about her friend to be afraid?

2  *Salvius' plot*. Where do you think he has gained his knowledge of Domitia's character and likely behaviour? Do you think his wife would have helped him to make use of her sister's house? What can you remember about her (last seen in Stage 14 entertaining Quintus, having removed the best furniture from Salvius' study in Britain to adorn the bedroom of the visitor)?

3  *Atmosphere*. How would you describe the atmosphere of this passage? Identify the words which create this effect. Does the title contribute to the effect? What English title would you give to the story? If you were filming or recording this story, what sound effects would you use?

4  *Roman house*. Put up a plan of a town house or ask students to sketch one (see Book I, p. 11) so that they can envisage the events in the stories on pp. 96-9.

## Consolidation

Set individual students or pairs to prepare about five lines each to translate. Make sure the whole story is covered. Discuss their translations in story order.

Ask students to pick out the nouns or pronouns described by the following participles, and explain the cases used: **missam** (line 3), **ēgressa** (line 6), **vecta** (line 9), **apertam** (line 12), **ingredientibus** (line 14), **vīsīs** (line 20). Discuss literal and idiomatic translations of the last two.

## īnsidiae II (pp. 97-8)

**Story**. Vitellia's bedroom is dark and Domitia sends her maid for a lamp. When she does not return and the bedroom is found empty, Domitia is panic-stricken. Encountering Paris as she runs through the atrium, she realises a trap has been set for them; they must escape while they can.

**First reading**. Read the story at one sitting, but use a variety of techniques to add to students' suspense and appreciation. For instance, handle lines 1-9 in a manner which conveys the mounting tension leading up to Domitia's realisation of the plot in **falsa erat epistula!**

1  Read in Latin **itaque ... ferret** (lines 1-4), leaving Domitia in the dark while you ask the class to tell you what has happened.

2  Then read **in silentiō ... nōn rediit** (lines 4-6). By stopping here you emphasise Domitia's total isolation in the dark house. Ask volunteers to translate. Give credit for the translation which best conveys the atmosphere.

3  **tandem ... vacuum erat** (lines 6-7). Contrast Domitia's impetuosity with the sudden threat presented by the word **vacuum**. Students will be eager to say what has happened. Check that they understand **morae impatiēns**.

4  In reading **tum dēmum ... epistula** (lines 7-9), build up the sense of mounting danger and the horrifying realisation contained in the last words. Elicit the meaning with questions.

After reading the remainder of the story, let students work out the meaning in pairs. Some may need help with **priusquam ... accideret** (line 11) and **īnsidiae ... parātae sunt** (line 15).

### Discussion

1 The empress sets out with a team of litter bearers and her maid. Ask students to identify the stages by which she becomes increasingly isolated: **servīs ... relictīs** (Part I, line 13), **Chionēn remīsit** (Part II, line 4), **vacuum erat** (Part II, line 7).

2 What do you think is the climax of the story?

3 **dum redīret** (line 5). This is the first occurrence of **dum** with the subjunctive. Students are quite likely to say 'She waited until the slave-girl returned'. Do not comment, but let them go on to the next sentence "But she did not return') and then invite amendments to the original sentence. 'What was she waiting for?' will help if students have difficulty. Point out the contrast between the indicative, used for facts, and the subjunctive often used for 'not-quite-facts', and then go on to explain the subjunctive in **priusquam ... accideret** (line 11). A previous example of **priusquam** with the subjunctive occurred in **Tychicus**, p. 79, line 9, and there are further examples of **dum** and **priusquam** on p. 139.

### Consolidation

Students might enjoy telling this story as Domitia, reproducing what she did and felt in the empty house. Others (if there is time) might like to present the scene with creepy musical and other sound effects at appropriate moments.

## ** exitium I (p. 98)

**Story**. Myropnous warns Paris and Domitia of the Praetorian Guard's approach. While they flee to the back gate, he blocks the front door with furniture and, setting fire to it, turns to follow them.

**First reading**. Keep a good pace by reading the story through in Latin and eliciting the meaning by comprehension questions as you go, without formal translation. This is especially helpful with the more complex sentences: **Domitia ... contendit** (lines 1-2); **quō factō ... coepit** (lines 11-13).

### Discussion

1 Who were the Praetorian Guard? Does it surprise you that Epaphroditus was able to command the emperor's bodyguard?

2 What effect is achieved by breaking the sentences into short phrases? What features of language create this effect (e.g. ablative absolutes, participial phrases, **neque** reiterated, etc.)?

3 Do you expect Domitia, Paris and Myropnous to escape?

Note: 'About the language I' follows well here. See p. 77 of this Guide for teaching suggestions.

**Consolidation**. Check that students recognise the form and meaning of imperatives: **prohibē** (line 8) and prohibitions: **nōlī dēspērāre** (line 7) and give further practice if necessary.

Pick out the examples of present participles: **dīcente** (line 1), **haesitantēs** (line 15), **pulsantium** (line 17), **flagrante** (line 19) and ask students for idiomatic translations in context, together with the case, number and gender.

## exitium II (pp. 98-9)

**Story**. Finding two soldiers guarding the back gate, Paris entices them inside so that Domitia can escape. Trapped in the garden, he makes for the roof but loses his footing. Hearing him crash, Domitia returns and is arrested lamenting over his dead body.

**First reading**. Recall the events of **exitium I** by putting up some short key sentences and asking for translation and comment. Take **exitium II** in three parts, reading each section aloud in Latin and exploring it with comprehension questions, some with the class as a whole, some with students working in pairs or groups:

*Escape attempt, lines 1-12:*
    What discovery did Paris and Domitia make at the back gate (lines 1-2)?
    How did Domitia react to this (lines 2-3)? How did Paris behave (lines 3-4)?
    Why did Paris dart out before dashing back into the garden (lines 4-6)?
    What did the soldiers shout?
    How did he baffle the soldiers? Why did he mock them (lines 9-10)?

*Fate of Paris, lines 13-22:*
    What noise did Paris hear (lines 13-14)?
    What made him realise the extent of his danger (line 15)?
    Where did Paris leap from? Where to? Would you expect Paris to have a good
        chance of making the leap? (lines 18-20)
    What went wrong (lines 21-2)?

*Fate of Domitia, lines 23-31.*
    What had Domitia done while Paris was distracting the soldiers? Why had she
        not run away? (lines 23-4)
    Why did she return to the garden (lines 24-7)?
    What caused her to give herself away (lines 27-9)?
    How did the tribune complete his mission (lines 30-1)?

**Discussion**
1    Why was Paris so popular? How would you describe his character? Can you think of anyone comparable in the modern world of entertainment?
2    What will probably happen to Domitia? Can students remember details of Salvius' promise to Epaphroditus (p. 94, line 16)? Note: Domitian's suspicions about Paris and Domitia, Paris' death in AD 83, and a divorce between Domitian and Domitia are recorded by the historians Suetonius and Dio Cassius. The details in this Stage are fictitious. Subsequently, after the divorce, Domitian took his niece Julia as his mistress. Domitia was restored in AD 84, and both she and Julia lived with him. When Domitian was murdered in AD 96, Domitia may have known about the plot to kill him.

## Consolidation

Divide students into groups of three or four, and allocate to each group one section of the story to translate and explore, listing some features of language to find and explain, e.g.:

*Lines 1-12*: superlative adjective, verb in the subjunctive, ablative absolute.

*Lines 13-22*: present participle, verb in subjunctive, deponent verb.

*Lines 23-31*: deponent verb, verb in the subjunctive, ablative absolute.

Ask the groups to share their work, and clear up any difficulties. Then focus on the longer sentences (lines 2-4, 4-6, 23-4, 26-7, 27-8), asking comprehension questions similar to those on p. 140, which provide an opportunity for further practice. Some sentences lend themselves to the type of analysis suggested on p. 16 of this Guide.

**Illustration**. Paris is posing behind the statue in order to hide from the Praetorian Guard. Ask students to pick out the Latin sentence that best describes the picture.

## About the language 1: present passive infinitive (p. 100)

**New language feature**. The present passive infinitive, and the present infinitive of deponent verbs.

**Discussion**. Read paragraphs 1-3 with the class, and set them to translate the examples in paragraph 4. In going over their work, ask 'What seems to be the usual difference between the present active infinitive and the present passive infinitive?'. If necessary, draw attention to the 3rd conjugation by asking them which passive infinitive differs from the other three.

Introduce paragraph 5 by asking students to translate a familiar sentence, e.g.:

difficile est eīs per viās prōgredī (p. 96, line 10)

Domitia ad aulam ... regredī cōnstituit (p. 97, line 10)

After completing paragraph 5, ask students to demonstrate from the examples how the deponent infinitive is like a passive infinitive ('it ends in -ī'), and then how it is like an active infinitive ('it means 'to ...', not 'to be ...-ed').

## Consolidation

Ask students to identify and translate in context the five passive and deponent infinitives on p. 98, **exitium I: vidērī** (line 4), **ingredī** (line 9), **ēlābī** (line 10), **effringī** (line 16), **sequī** (line 19). Make sure that students can recognise deponent verbs in the Vocabulary by studying p. 142, paragraphs 3-5.

## honōrēs (p. 101)

**Story**. Congratulating Salvius, Epaphroditus describes Domitia's fate, the plans for public celebrations, and the emperor's promise to give Salvius a consulship. Overhearing this, Myropnous realises Salvius' part in Paris' death and breaks his pipes, swearing not to play again until Salvius is dead.

**First reading**. Introduce the story by picking out with the class and putting on the board all the promises that were made by Epaphroditus and Salvius in **ultiō Epaphrodītī** (p. 94):

praemium tibi dabitur (line 10).

ego tibi tōtam rem administrābō (line 12).

īnsidiae parābuntur; Domitia et Paris ... ēlicientur; ambō capientur et pūnientur (lines 13-14).

Domitia accūsābitur; damnābitur; fortasse relēgābitur (line 16).

(Paris) ēmovēbitur (line 19).

Ask students to cross off the promises which they know have so far been fulfilled.

Read lines 1-19 of **honōrēs** in Latin and ask students what they have understood from your reading. Then set them to translate the passage in pairs and find out if the list of promises has now been completely fulfilled. Be prepared to help them with the initial dative in line 1, and see how well they cope with the change of tenses in Epaphroditus' speech.

The mood of lines 20-6 is quite different. Explore it with comprehension questions and then work out with the group the most powerful translation of the first and last sentences, noting in particular the word order of lines 20-1.

### Discussion
1 Why do you think there were to be public celebrations?
2 What reward did Epaphroditus expect? What privileges would he gain by this (see p. 109)? Would it make him popular with nobly-born senators?
3 What reward was Salvius promised? Who told him? Is there anything odd in this? (Salvius held the consulship some time before AD 86.)
4 What do you think is the likelihood of Myropnous being able to take vengeance on Salvius?
5 Do you think the title for this Stage is appropriate?

### Consolidation
Ask for an oral translation of lines 7-9 (**puerī ... offerent**), making sure that students recognise the future active. Then to do exercise 1 in 'Practising the language'.

Ask for a written translation of Epaphroditus' speech as an introduction to completing 'About the language 2'.

**Illustration.** Late 2nd century tombstone in Florence. The figure is shown with double pipes. The inscription in Greek reads:

| THEOIS K | *To the gods and ......* |
|---|---|
| MYROPNOUI NANO | *Myropnous dwarf* |
| CHORAULE | *player for a chorus of singers and dancers* |

## About the language 2: future passive tense (p. 102)

**New language feature.** Future passive, 3rd person singular and plural.

**Discussion.** This is a straightforward note which also offers the opportunity to reinforce the characteristics of deponent verbs. Take it in two parts, paragraphs 1-3 and 4 with consolidation after each part.

**Consolidation.** After completing paragraphs 1-3, turn back to p. 94 and set students to identify verbs in the future tense in lines 7-19 and say whether they are active or passive. Similarly, after paragraph 4, ask students to pick out the future tenses on p. 101, lines 1-19, and say whether they are active, passive or deponent.

# Word patterns: compound verbs 3 (p. 103)

**New language feature.** Compounds with the prefix **ad-, con-, prō-, trāns-** and **per-**.

**Discussion.** Let students work through this independently or in groups and share their observations.

## Practising the language (pp. 104-5)

*Exercise 1.* Complete the sentences by selecting the correct person of the future active.
*Exercise 2.* Translate English sentences into Latin with words chosen from a selection.
*Exercise 3.* Translate active sentences and convert to passive form.

### Illustrations
- The consular symbols, drawings based on Roman coins. The fasces, a bundle of rods tied with a red thong, was carried before a senior magistrate by a lictor. A consul had twelve lictors. The axe in each bundle was carried only outside Rome. The folding ivory **sella cūrūlis** was the chair of office on which a senior magistrate sat when conducting official business.
- Small bronze statuette of a wreathed lictor holding the fasces (*British Museum*).

## Cultural background material (pp. 106-9)

**Content.** This section extends the information about freedmen (including the manumission ceremony) given in Book I, Stage 6, and incorporates some tomb inscriptions and a section on imperial freedmen.

**Discussion.** The following questions could be used for clarification or discussion, or as a guide for students to make their own notes:
1 How would you define a freedman?
2 Why might a master choose to free a slave? (see also Stage 6: financial reasons, slave too old or infirm to work, slave freed at master's death, slave could buy freedom, freedom given as the result of a special act like saving the master's life, etc.)
3 What privileges were open to a Roman freedman?
4 What constraints limited a Roman freedman?
5 What were the obligations of (a) the ex-master (b) the ex-slave to each other?
6 What led to some freedmen (usually not those who had been unskilled workers) becoming wealthy and successful?
7 Why did some freedmen prefer to stay with their masters?
8 What was special about **lībertī Augustī**? What powers and privileges did they have? How were they viewed by Roman senators?

The inscriptions on p. 108 are as follows:
1 In memory of Titus Flavius Homerus, a well-deserving ex-master, Titus Flavius Hyacinthus (erected this tomb).
2 In memory of Julius Vitalis, a well-deserving freedman, his ex-master (erected this tomb).
3 Titus Flavius Eumolpus and Flavia Quinta built (this tomb) for themselves, their freedmen and freedwomen and their descendants.

**4** Titus Flavius Cerialis erected (this tomb) in memory of Flavia Philaenis his well-deserving freedwoman and wife.

### Illustrations

p. 106 •  Relief (*Musée Royale du Mariemont*). A magistrate is touching the kneeling slave with a rod. A slave already freed (left) is shaking hands with a fourth person, probably his master. The kneeling figure is a slave bowing to his master after receiving his freedom. Both slaves are wearing the pilleus, showing that they have been freed.

p. 107 •  Hall of the Augustales. The shrine in the recess on the right would have held a statue, and there are two statue bases at the foot of the pillars, all for statues of members of the imperial family, used as a focus for worship. The wall paintings feature Hercules, legendary founder of Herculaneum. Evidence for ceremonial dinners is found in inscriptions.

•  Inscription from a tomb outside the Nuceria Gate, Pompeii, put up by Publius Vesonius, freedman, during his lifetime for himself and his patroness, wife of his former master. The photograph shows the left hand column, and part of the central column, of three columns. It reads:

| | |
|---|---|
| P VESONIVS ) L(IBERTVS) | VESONIAE |
| PHILEROS [AVGVSTALIS] | PATRONAE |
| VIVOS MONVMENT(VM) | |
| FECIT SIBI ET [SVIS] | |

*P(ublius) Vesonius Phileros, Caius' freedman, [Augustalis], while still alive made this monument for himself and [his family] and his patroness Vesonia.*

The letter before L (line 1) is an alternative form of C. VIVOS is an alternative form of VIVVS. The words in square brackets were obviously squashed in later, suggesting that Vesonius became an Augustalis and gained his own household after the inscription was completed

p. 109 •  Courtyard in the private quarters of Domitian's palace, surrounded by two-storey buildings. For the location of the palace see pp. 1 and 43.

p. 110 •  Obverse of aureus of Domitian (*private collection*). Inscription: IMP(ERATOR) CAES(AR) DOMIT(IANVS) AVG(VSTVS) GERM(ANICVS) P(ONTIFEX) M(AXIMVS) TR(IBVNICIA) P(OTESTAS) VI , meaning: *Emperor Caesar Domitianus Augustus Germanicus, High Priest, holder of Tribunician Power six times.*

p. 111 •  Reverse of bronze sestertius, showing Domitia and her infant son, who later died (*British Museum*). Inscription: MATRI DIVI CAESAR(IS) S(ENATVS) C(ONSVLTO), meaning *To the mother of the divine Caesar by the senate's command* (note that **senātus** is a 4th declension noun).

## Checklist vocabulary: cognates and compounds

auctōritās, gaudēre, mors, precēs, suspiciō.

## Suggested activities

1 Devise a funerary monument for Clemens, set up by his ex-master Quintus, with an inscription based on the formulae used in those on p. 108.

2 Prepare for Test 2. Suggestions for students:

  a From each Stage in the book choose one story to re-read carefully, asking for help with any sentences or phrases you find difficult;

  b Read through the model sentences, and the 'About the language' sections; select some of the examples to translate and ask for help with any difficulties;

  c Look over any work you have done on the cultural background, noting carefully the comments and advice you have received.

# Language synopsis of Book IV

This synopsis follows the same plan and is designed for the same purposes as the Book I language synopsis described on p. 92 of the Book I Teacher's Guide. When reading a Stage with a class, teachers are strongly advised to concentrate on the features dealt with in that Stage's language note(s), rather than attempting discussion and analysis of other features listed here. LI = Language information section.

| Stage | Language feature | Place of language note, etc. |
|---|---|---|
| 29 | 3rd person singular and plural, present and imperfect passive | 29, LI |
| | purpose clause with **quī** and **ubi** | 29, LI |
| | purpose clause and indirect command with **nē** | 31, LI |
| | ablative + verb (e.g. **flammīs cōnsūmēbantur**) | |
| | adjectival **is** and pronominal **hic** | LI |
| | **dum** + present indicative | |
| 30 | perfect and pluperfect passive (all persons) | 30, LI |
| | genitive of present participle used substantivally (e.g. **sonitum pulsantium**) | |
| | further ablative usages (e.g. **uxōrem nōbilissimā gente nātam, ārea strepitū plēna**) | |
| 31 | ablative absolute | 31, LI |
| | purpose clause and indirect command with **nē** (from Stage 29) | 31, LI |
| | dative noun + participle at beginning of sentence | LI |
| 32 | deponent verbs | 32, LI |
| | gerundive of obligation with transitive verbs | 32, LI |
| | future participle (met from Stage 26) | 32, LI |
| | double indirect question with **necne** | |
| 33 | future and future perfect active (all persons) | 33, LI |
| | future of **sum** (all persons) | 33, LI |
| | **priusquam** + subjunctive | LI |
| | ablative of description | LI |
| | conditional clauses (indicative) | |
| 34 | present passive infinitive (including deponent) | 34, LI |
| | 3rd person singular and plural, future passive (including deponent) | 34, LI |
| | **dum** + subjunctive | LI |

The following terms are used in Book IV. Numerals indicate the Stage in which each term is first used.

| | |
|---|---|
| active | 29* |
| passive | 29* |
| compound verb | 29 |
| ablative absolute | 31 |
| deponent | 32 |
| future | 33* |
| future perfect | 33 |
| diminutive | 33 |
| present active infinitive | 34 |
| present passive infinitive | 34 |

*The terms 'active', 'passive' and 'future' have been used earlier (in Stages 22, 21 and 32 respectively) in connection with participles.

# APPENDIX A: ATTAINMENT TESTS

For notes on the purpose of the attainment tests, and suggestions for their use, see Book I Teacher's Guide, p. 95. The words in bold type are either new to students or have occurred infrequently in the reading material. A few new words with obvious meanings are not printed in bold type.

## Test 1

This test should be worked after the class has finished Stage 31.

**senex**

### I: Written translation

Teachers may like to set the scene for this story by referring to the picture on p. 1.

in Viā Sacrā prope amphitheātrum Flāviam stābat senex
**pauperrimus**. vultus eius **pallidus** erat, tunica sordida, pedēs **nūdī**.
parvam **cistam** manū tenēbat in quā pauca **sulphurāta** posita erant.
    'sulphurāta! sulphurāta!' exclāmāvit vōce **raucā**.
    ingēns Rōmānōrum multitūdō eum **praeterībat**: senātōrēs, multīs         5
**comitantibus** clientibus, ad **cūriam** contendēbant ut **ōrātiōnem**
Imperātōris audīrent; **ōrātōrēs** ad **basilicam**, sacerdōtēs ad templa
ībant; fēminae dīvitēs ad vīllās **lectīcīs** vehēbantur; mercātōrēs per
viam prōcēdentēs ab amīcīs salūtābantur; servī, ingentēs **sarcinās**
portantēs, ā dominīs **incitābantur**. omnēs, negōtiō occupātī, clāmōrēs     10
senis neglegēbant.
    tandem sōle **occidente** senex ad flūmen īre cōnstituit ut locum
quaereret ubi dormīret. cum Subūram trānsīret, subitō iuvenis **ēbrius**,
ē tabernā cum duōbus servīs ēgressus, eī obstitit.
    iuvenis 'sceleste!' inquit. 'nōlī iuvenem nōbilem impedīre.'     15
    tum servīs imperāvit ut senem verberārent. senex, ā servīs
verberātus, humī **dēcidit exanimātus**.

### II: Comprehension test

senex tandem **sē recēpit**. cum sulphurāta humī dispersa quaereret,
**crumēnam**, quae ā iuvene **omissa erat**, cōnspexit. crumēna dēnāriīs
plēna erat. senex magnō **gaudiō** affectus est. tabernam ingressus
**caupōnem** iussit cēnam splendidam parāre.
    senex, cēnā cōnsūmptā, ad flūmen prōgressus prope pontem     5
**Fabricium cōnsēdit**. dēnāriōs ē crumēnā extractōs **identidem**
laetissimus **numerābat**. dēnique, cum crumēnam summā cūrā
cēlāvisset nē fūrēs eam invenīrent, obdormīvit.
    quamquam fessus erat, nōn sēcūrus dormiēbat. nam **in somnīs** sē
vidēbat in basilicā stantem; ab illō iuvene **fūrtī** accūsābātur; tum     10
**convictus** et ad mortem damnātus, ad carcerem trahēbātur; subitō ē

somnō excitātus est, vehementer tremēns. adeō perterritus erat ut
pecūniam, quam nūper comparāverat, **abicere** cōnstitueret. itaque ad
flūmen prōgressus, crumēnā in aquam abiectā,

'multō melius est', inquit, 'pauper esse et sēcūrus dormīre quam     15
dīves esse et poenās timēre.'

diē **illūcēscente**, ad Viam Sacram regressus, 'sulphurāta!
sulphurāta!' exclāmāvit.

multī cīvēs eum praeterībant; aliī clāmōrēs eius neglegēbant; aliī
eum vituperābant; nūllī sulphurāta ēmērunt. ille autem vītam     20
miserrimam sēcūrus agēbat.

| | |
|---|---|
| sulphurāta, n. pl. | *matches* |
| crumēnam: crumēna | *purse* |

## Questions

1  What did the old man catch sight of? How did it come to be
    there?                                                            2
.2  Why was the old man particularly pleased?                         1
3  **tabernam ... parāre** (lines 3-4). What did he do as a result of
    his good fortune?                                                 2
4  **cēnā cōnsūmptā** (line 5). What did the old man do after this?   2
5  **identidem ... numerābat** (lines 6-7). Suggest a reason why
    the old man did this.                                             1
6  What did he do immediately before he fell asleep? Why?            2
7  **nam ... stantem** (lines 9-10). What did the old man see himself
    doing in his dream?                                               1
8  How was the young man involved?                                    1
9  **tum ... trahēbātur** (lines 10-11). What happened to the old
    man in the next part of the dream?                                3
10  Write down two Latin words that describe the effect of the
    dream on the old man. What did he decide to do?                   2
11  What reason did he give for his action?                           3
12  Where did he go at daybreak? Why?                                 2
13  Which was the only group of passers-by to make any response
    to him (lines 19-20)?                                             1
14  Which word in the last sentence sums up the old man's state
    of mind?                                                          1
15  Do you think the old man made the right decision? Give a
    reason.                                                           1

TOTAL 25

## Answers

The answers and mark scheme are as follows. Give credit for any sensible answer.

 1  A purse. It had been dropped by the young man/The young man had dropped it. .......................................................... 2
 2  The purse was full of denarii. ............................................... 1
 3  He entered an inn and ordered the innkeeper to prepare a splendid dinner. .................................................................... 2
 4  He went to the river and sat down near the Fabrician bridge. 2
 5  He could not believe his luck/It gave him great pleasure to do this *or similar*. ................................................................ 1
 6  He hid the purse with the utmost care/very carefully. ...... 1
     So that thieves should not find it. ...................................... 1
 7  Standing in a basilica/law court. ........................................ 1
 8  He was accusing the old man of theft/The old man was being accused of theft by him. ................................................... 1
 9  After being convicted and condemned to death he was being dragged to the prison. ......................................................... 3
10  *Either* **vehementer tremēns** *or* **tremēns** and **perterritus**. ....... 1
     He decided to throw away the money. ................................ 1
11  It was  much better to be poor and to sleep free from care than to be rich and fear punishment. ......................................... 3
12  To the Sacred Way; to sell his matches. ............................ 2
13  Those who cursed him. ........................................................ 1
14  **sēcūrus**. .............................................................................. 1
15  Yes:  A good conscience is better than guilt/constant worry/He might have been murdered for his money, etc.
     No:  The young man deserved to lose his money/The old man should have disregarded his dream/He was entitled to the money as compensation for the young man's assault on him, etc.
     *Give one mark for any good point.* ........................................ 1

TOTAL 25

Teachers may like to note how students are coping with the following features in particular:

> ablative with adjective: **negōtiō occupātī** (I, 10); **crumēna dēnāriīs plēna erat** (II, 2-3).

> ablative with verbs: **manū tenēbat** (I, 3); **exclāmāvit vōce raucā** (I, 4); **lectīcīs vehēbantur** (I, 8); **summā cūrā cēlāvisset** (II, 7-8).

> ablative absolute: **multīs comitantibus clientibus** (I, 5-6); **sōle occidente** (I, 12); **cēnā cōnsūmptā** (II, 5); **crumēnā in aquam abiectā** (II, 14).

3rd person singular and plural imperfect passive: **fēminae ... vehēbantur** (I. 8); **mercātōrēs ... salūtābantur** (I, 8-9); **servī ... incitābantur** (I, 9-10); **trahēbātur** (II, 11).

3rd person singular perfect passive: **excitātus est** (II, 12).

3rd person singular and plural pluperfect passive: **sulphurāta posita erant** (I, 3); **quae ... omissa erat** (II, 2).

**nē** with subjunctive: **nē ... invenīrent** (II, 8).

**ubi** with subjunctive: **ubi dormīret** (I, 13).

**nōlī** with infinitive: **nōlī ... impedīre** (I, 15).

omission of first of two verbs: **ōrātōrēs ... ībant** (I, 7-8).

'branching': **tandem ... dormīret** (I, 12-13); **dēnique ... obdormīvit** (II, 7-8).

'nesting': **adeō ... cōnstitueret** (II, 12-13).

# Test 2

This test should be worked after the class has finished Stage 34.

## Agathyrsus et Cordus

### I: Introduction; for oral translation

erat prope amphitheātrum Flāvium **īnsula** altissima, quam aedificāverat lībertus dīves, Agathyrsus nōmine. in hāc īnsulā erant **conclāvia spatiōsa** et splendida ubi Agathyrsus ipse habitābat: **parietēs marmore** ōrnātī erant; ubīque stābant statuae pretiōsae quae ex Graeciā importātae erant.　　　　　　　　　　　　　　　　　　5

　　in aliīs īnsulae partibus habitābant hominēs multō pauperiōrēs quam Agathysus. pauperrimus omnium erat poēta, Cordus nōmine, quī in **cēnāculō** sordidō sub **tēctō sitō** habitābat. tam pauper erat ut nihil habēret nisi lectum parvum paucōsque librōs. vīta eius erat difficillima: **quotiēns pluerat**, aqua in cēnāculum penetrābat. eum　　10
versūs scrībentem **vīcīnī clāmōribus** vexābant. eō absente, **mūrēs** librōs **dēvorābant.**

### II: Written translation

ōlim Cordus, in **cēnāculō** iacēns, versūs scrībere cōnābātur. subitō magnus **strepitus** in īnsulā **ortus est.** ille, quī clāmōrēs **vīcīnōrum** audīre solēbat, strepitum neglēxit quod intentē scrībēbat. mox tamen maiōre strepitū audītō, ad **fenestram** iit; **prōspiciēns** spectāculum terribile vīdit: tōta īnsula flammīs cōnsūmēbātur. vīcīnī, ex īnsulīs　　5
proximīs ēgressī, in viam conveniēbant. quī, simulac Cordum cōnspicātī sunt,

'fuge, Corde! fuge!' exclāmāvērunt. 'moritūrus es! nisi statim
dēscenderis, flammae tē dēvorābunt.'

quibus clāmōribus audītīs, Cordus quam celerrimē dēscendit. tōta       10
īnsula **fūmō** iam complēbātur. tam dēnsus erat fūmus ut nihil vidērī
posset. Cordus, quamquam vix **spīrāre** poterat, in viam effūgit, ubi
ingēns turba convēnerat. mediā in turbā, Agathyrsus, vultū sevērō,
imperābat servīs ut flammās exstinguerent. aliī, iussīs neglēctīs, pavōre
commōtī per viās fugiēbant; aliī immōtī stābant, **incertī** quid facerent;   15
aliī ad proximās īnsulās currēbant ut aquam peterent; nulla tamen aqua
comparārī poterat. mox tōta īnsula flammīs cōnsūmpta est.

## III: Comprehension test

amīcī Agathyrsī, cum audīvissent quid accidisset, ad eum
contendērunt. omnēs spē favōris dōna magnifica eī dedērunt. paucīs
diēbus, Agathyrsus tot statuās, pictūrās, mēnsās, lectōs accēpit ut
plūra habēret quam anteā. mox in eō locō ubi īnsula sita erat domum
novam splendidamque aedificārī iussit. dōna, quae ab amīcīs data          5
erant, per conclāvia **disposuit**.

Cordus tamen, librīs lectōque incēnsīs, nūllam pecūniam habēbat
neque ūlla dōna adeptus est. cum quondam per urbem miserrimus
**errāret**, servō Agathyrsī **occurrit**.

'nōnne dē Agathrysī scelere audīvistī?' inquit servus. 'ipse            10
īnsulam **cōnsultō** incendit ut domum magnificam eōdem in locō sibi
aedificāret. tot dōna accēpit ut tōtam domum splendidē ōrnāre
posset. ēheu! fortūna scelestīs favet.'

quibus rēbus audītīs Cordus magnā īrā commōtus,

'nōnne Agathyrsus pūniendus est?' inquit. 'ego ipse tōtam rem        15
versibus meīs nārrābō; nēmō ab eō iterum dēcipiētur.'

itaque versūs dē scelere scrīptōs in omnibus partibus urbis
recitāvit. scelere iam patefactō, tam īrātī erant amīcī Agathyrsī ut ipsī
domum novam **noctū** incenderent.

## Questions

1  What did Agathyrsus' friends do when they heard the news
  (lines 1-2)?                                                       1
2  Which two words in the second sentence suggest their
  motive? Translate them.                                            2
3  **dōna magnifica** (line 2). What did these consist of?                    2
4  What order did Agathyrsus give about the site where the
  block of flats had stood (lines 4-5)?                              2
5  How did he furnish his house?                                              2
6  What possessions did Cordus lose in the fire (line 7)?                     1
7  Why could he not replace them?                                            2

8  How did Cordus come to meet Agathyrsus' slave?                1
 9  What crime was Agathyrsus guilty of?                           1
10  **fortūna scelestīs favet** (line 13). Who, in particular, was the
    slave thinking of? Why was this a suitable thing to say at
    this point?                                                    2
11  What was Cordus' reaction to the slave's information
    (line 14)?                                                     1
12  '**nōnne Agathyrsus pūniendus est?**' (line 15). How did Cordus
    propose to punish Agathyrsus? What did he say the result
    would be?                                                      4
13  **versūs dē scelere scrīptōs** (line 17). How did people get to
    know about these?                                              1
14  Who were angry? What action did they take? (lines 18-19)       2
15  Why do you think Agathyrsus was not content with his
    previous luxury flat? Give one reason.                         1
                                                          TOTAL 25

## Answers

The answers and mark scheme are as follows. Give credit for any sensible answer.

 1  They hurried to him.                                           1
 2  **spē favōris.** In the hope of (gaining) favour *or similar*. 2
 3  statues, pictures, tables, couches/beds.                       2
 4  He gave orders that a new and splendid house should be built
    there.                                                         2
 5  With the presents his friends had given.                       2
 6  His books and bed.                                             1
 7  He had no money and he did not get any presents.               2
 8  He met him when he was (very unhappily) wandering
    through the city (one day).                                    1
 9  Arson.                                                         1
10  Agathyrsus.                                                    1
    He had benefitted from his crime, while innocent
    people like Cordus had suffered/Agathyrsus had built his
    new mansion/He had furnished it with presents from his
    friends.                                                       1
11  He was very angry.                                             1
12  He said he himself would tell the whole story in his verse.    2
    No-one would be deceived by him (Agathyrsus) again.            2
13  Cordus recited the lines/verse (he had written about the
    crime) in all parts of the city.                               1
14  The friends of Agathyrsus.                                     1
    They burnt his new house by night.                             1

**15** Agathyrsus may have disliked rowdy/poor neighbours/bad
condition of insula/fire hazard/he may have wanted more
space, a different, more fashionable arrangement of rooms, etc.   1

TOTAL <u>25</u>

Teachers may like to note how students are coping with the following features in particular:

> verbs: imperfect tense of deponents: **cōnābātur** (II, 1);
>
>> perfect tense of deponents: **ortus est** (II, 2); **cōnspicātī sunt** (II, 6-7); **adeptus est** (III, 8);
>>
>> imperfect passive: **cōnsūmēbātur** (II, 5); **complēbātur** (II, 11);
>>
>> perfect passive: **cōnsūmpta est** (II, 17);
>>
>> pluperfect passive: **ōrnātī erant** (I, 4); **importātae erant** (I, 5); **data erant** (III, 5-6);
>>
>> present infinitive passive: **vidērī** (II, 11); **comparārī** (II, 17); **aedificārī** (III, 5);
>>
>> future and future perfect active: **dēvorābunt** (II, 9); **nārrābō** (III, 16); **dēscenderis** (II, 9);
>>
>> future passive: **dēcipiētur** (III, 16).
>
> ablative absolute: **eō absente** (I, 11); **maiōre strepitū audītō** (II, 4); **quibus clāmōribus audītīs** (II, 10); **iussīs neglēctīs** (II, 14); **librīs lectōque incēnsīs** (III, 7); **scelere iam patefactō** (III, 18).
>
> connecting relative: **quī ... exclāmāvērunt** (II, 6-8); **quibus clāmōribus audītīs** (II, 10).
>
> accusative + nominative + verb: **eum ... vexābant** (I, 10-11).

# APPENDIX B:

# BOOK IV VOCABULARY CHECKLIST

accūsāre (34)
adhūc (30)
adipīscī (34)
adversus (32)
   rēs adversae (32)
aequus (32)
afficere (30)
   affectus (30)
aliī ... aliī (29)
altus (31)
ambō (30)
ante (31)
appellāre (33)
ascendere (29)
at (33)
auctor (34)
   mē auctōre (34)
audācia (29)

brevis (33)

captīvus (29)
circumvenīre (29)
comitārī (34)
compōnere (32)
cōnārī (34)
   cōnātus (32)
conicere (33)
cōnsistere (31)
cōnspicārī (34)
cōnsulere (30)
contrā (33)
convertere (32)
crās (33)

dēcidere (33)
dēfendere (29)
dēmittere (30)
dēscendere (33)
dīrus (29)

dīves (30)
dīvitiae (30)
dolor (29)
dum (34)
dux (31)

effundere (32)
ēgredī (34)
ēicere (33)
et ... et (33)
excipere (33)

frangere (34)
frūmentum (31)
fuga (33)

gaudium (34)
gēns (30)

haud (34)
haudquāquam (31)
hīc (33)
hortārī (34)

īdem (31)
identidem (31)
ignōscere (32)
incēdere (29)
ingredī (34)
iniūria (30)

labor (32)
līberī (29)
lībertās (32)
loquī (34)
lūdus (33)
lūx (29)

magnopere (30)
mālle (29)

mēnsa (32)
modo (34)
morī (34)
movēre (33)

nāscī (34)
   nātus (30)
nē (31)
nē ... quidem (32)
nec (32)
   nec ... nec (32)
neglegere (31)
nimis (30)
nisi (33)
nōbilis (30)
numerus (33)

ōdī (29)
omnīnō (30)
opprimere (32)
opus (30)
ōrāre (31)
ōtiōsus (32)

patī (34)
pauper (32)
pavor (30)
perficere (29)
populus (29)
potestās (33)
precārī (34)
prius (29)
priusquam (34)
procul (34)
proficīscī (34)
   profectus (32)
prōgredī (34)
   prōgressus (31)

quārē? (30)
quasi (34)
quia (33)
quīdam (32)

rapere (31)
reficere (33)
rēgīna (33)
regredī (34)

salūs (29)
saxum (30)
scelus (29)
scindere (31)
secāre (30)

sequī (34)
  secūtus (32)
sine (34)
sōl (30)
sonitus (34)
soror (30)
spērāre (31)
spernere (29)
subvenīre (32)
superbus (31)
suspicārī (34)

tempus (31)
timor (30)

ubīque (29)
undique (31)
utrum (33)

vehere (31)
vel (34)
vērus (33)
  rē vērā (33)
vester (29)
vestīmenta (34)
vincīre (31)
vīvus (29)
volvere (31)
vultus (31)

# BIBLIOGRAPHY

## Books

Books marked * are suitable for students. Some of the others would also be suitable for students to refer to under the teacher's guidance. Some out-of-print (OP) books are included in case teachers possess them or can obtain second-hand copies.

Adam, J-P. *Roman Building: Materials and Techniques* (Routledge, pbk, 1999)

Augarde, A.J. *The Oxford Guide to Word Games* (OUP, new edition, 2003)

Balsdon, J.P.V.D. *Life and Leisure in Ancient Rome* (Bodley Head, 1969, OP)

> *Roman Women* (Barnes and Noble, 1983, OP)

Barrow, R.H. *The Romans* (Pelican, new edn, 1990)

Barton, I.M, (ed.) *Roman Public Buildings* (University of Exeter Press, pbk, 1995)

> *Roman Domestic Buildings* (University of Exeter Press, pbk, 1996)

Beacham, R.C. *The Roman Theatre and its Audience* (Routledge, pbk, 1995)

> *Spectacle Entertainments of Early Imperial Rome* (Yale UP, 1999)

Bonechi Colour Guides *All of Ancient Rome* (new edn, 1992)

Bowman, A.K., Champlin, E. and Lintott, A.W. (eds) *Cambridge Ancient History, Volume X, The Augustan Empire, 43 BC - 69 AD* (CUP, new edn, 1996)

Bradley, K.R. *Slaves and Masters in the Roman Empire* (CUP, pbk, 1988)

> *Slavery and Society at Rome* (CUP, pbk, 1994)

Carcopino, J. *Daily Life in Ancient Rome* (Penguin, new edn, 1991)

Carter, A. *Themes for Classical Studies* (58 photocopiable mastersheets) (CUP, 1991)

Claridge, A. *Rome*. Oxford Archaeological Guides (OUP, pbk, 1998)

Connolly, P. and Dodge, H. *The Ancient City: Life in Classical Athens and Rome* (OUP, 1998)

> *The Holy Land* (OUP, 1999)

Crook, J.A. *Law and Life of Rome* (Cornell UP, 1984)

Dudley, D.R. *Roman Society* (Penguin, 1991)

Grant, M. *The World of Rome* (Phoenix Press, new edn, 2000)

Hamey, L.A. and Hamey, J.A. *Roman Engineers* (CUP, 1981)

Hill, D.R. *A History of Engineering in Classical and Medieval Times* (Routledge, pbk, 1996)

Hodges, H.W.M. *Artifacts* (Duckworth, pbk, 1989)

Hornblower, S. and Spawforth, A. (eds) *Oxford Classical Dictionary* (OUP, 3rd edn, 1997)

Landels, J.G. *Engineering in the Ancient World* (Constable, new edn, 1998)

Lee, G. (trans.) *Ovid in Love* (John Murray, 2000)

Lewis, N. and Reinhold, M. *Roman Civilisation: A Sourcebook, II The Empire* (Columbia UP, 1990)

Loane, H.J. *Industry and Commerce of the City of Rome, 50 BC - 200 AD* (Porcupine Press, UK, 1980)

Macaulay, D. *City: A Story of Roman Planning and Construction* (Houghton Mifflin, 1983, OP)

Macdonald, W.L. *The Architecture of the Roman Empire* (Yale UP, new edn, 1988)

*The Pantheon: Design, Meaning and Progeny* (Harvard UP, pbk, 1990)

Martin, P. and Pulley, R. *The Roman World from Republic to Empire* (CUP, 1992)

McKay, A.G. *Houses, Villas and Palaces in the Roman World* (John Hopkins UP, 1998)

McKeever, S. *Ancient Rome* (Dorling Kindersley, 1995). An excellent little book to take on school trips.

Meiggs, R. *Roman Ostia* (Sandpiper Books, 1985)

Melville, A.D. (trans.) Ovid, *The Love Poems* (Oxford World Classics, pbk, 1998)

Paoli, U.E. *Rome, its People, Life and Customs* ((BCP, 1990)

Robinson, O.F. *Ancient Rome: City Planning and Administration* (Routledge, new edn, 1994)

Sandbach, F. H. *The Stoics* (BCP, new edn, 1989)

Scarre, C. *Penguin Historical Atlas of Ancient Rome* (Penguin, 1995)

Sims, L. *A Visitor's Guide to Ancient Rome* (Usborne, 1999)

Sisson, C.J. (trans.) Virgil, *Aeneid* (Everyman, 1998)

Southern, P. *Domitian, Tragic Tyrant* (Routledge, 1997)

Taylor, D. *The Greek and Roman Stage* (Duckworth, 1999)

*Roman Society* (Duckworth, 1998)

Tingay, G.I.F. and Badcock, J. *These Were the Romans* (Duckworth, new edn, 1998)

West, D. (trans.) Virgil, *Aeneid* (Penguin Classics, rev. edn, 2003)

Wheeler, Sir M. *Roman Art and Architecture* (Thames and Hudson, pbk, 1964)

Williamson, G.A. (trans.) and Smallwood, E.M. (ed.) Josephus, *The Jewish War* (Penguin, 1981)

Yadin, Y. *Masada* (Sphere, pbk, 1978, OP)

## Audio-Visual Resources

The Cambridge School Classics Project website: www.cambridgescp.com lists websites and other resources relevant to the content of Book IV.

### Slides and filmstrips

**Ministrips** R.L. Dalladay, Abbey Cottage, East Cliff, Whitby YO22 4JT.

*Forum Romanum.* 25 slides, notes (C21)

*Circus Maximus.* 16 slides, notes, reading commentary compiled from contemporary sources (C22)

*Colosseum.* 20 slides, notes (C24)

*The Corn Supply.* 16 slides, notes (C41)

*Aqueducts and Water Supply.* 30 slides, notes (C43)

*Faiths from the East.* 25 slides, notes; includes Mithras and Christianity (C15)

For further details and other titles in the series, send for the Ministrip catalogue, available from the address above.